THE MONEY TREE

SKETCHES OF LIFE IN UGANDA AT THE TURN OF THE MILLENNIUM

INGRID PASTEUR

SUGARBROOK BOOKS

Date of Publication
February 2002

Published by:
Sugarbrook Books,
Sugarbrook Manor,
Bromsgrove,
B60 3AT

Copyright 2002 Ingrid Pasteur

Printed by:
Proprint
Riverside Cottage
Great NorthRoad
Stibbington
Peterborough PE8 6LR

IBSN: 0-9541858-0-3

ACKNOWLEDGEMENTS

My sincerest thanks go to
Everyone who contributed in any way
to making this book happen;
Especially to
My Family for encouraging me to undertake the adventure
which inspired it;
The People in Uganda who shared their lives with me;
Tom Stacey, Belinda Morse and Beth Miller
who read and commented usefully on the text;
David for producing the cover design and map
on his computer and
several of my family for proof reading;
PROPRINT who were helpful and quick
with the printing.

CONTENTS

	Map	
1.	Why Uganda?	1
2.	The Money Tree	5
3.	The Children	13
4.	Lament of the Mango Tree	21
5.	Elections	22
6.	The Feast of St. Matthias Kalemba	26
7.	Paul's Bicycle	29
8.	Rachel's Student Days	35
9.	My Car	44
10.	Prelude to Malaria	49
11.	Ruth's Enterprise	53
12.	Swamp Baptism	57
13.	Banana Tree	62
14.	Annet's Dilemma	63
15.	Schools	68
16.	Noises in the Night	75
17.	Murchison Falls	81
18.	Alice's Duplicity	88
19.	Christmas in Kinkizi	97
20.	Susan's Hardship	104
21.	The Cardinal's Visit	109
22.	Wedding and Aftermath	113
23.	Joe's Persistence	118
24.	Encounters with the Police	128
25.	The Swallows	131
26.	Martha's Training	133
27.	Rukungiri Christmas	143
28.	Nightmare Journey	150
29.	A Death	152
30.	James and his Grandmother's Funeral	156
31.	Trees	159
32.	Karamoja	164
33.	Rachel's Later Problems	169
34.	Unfinished Finale	174
	Glossary	178

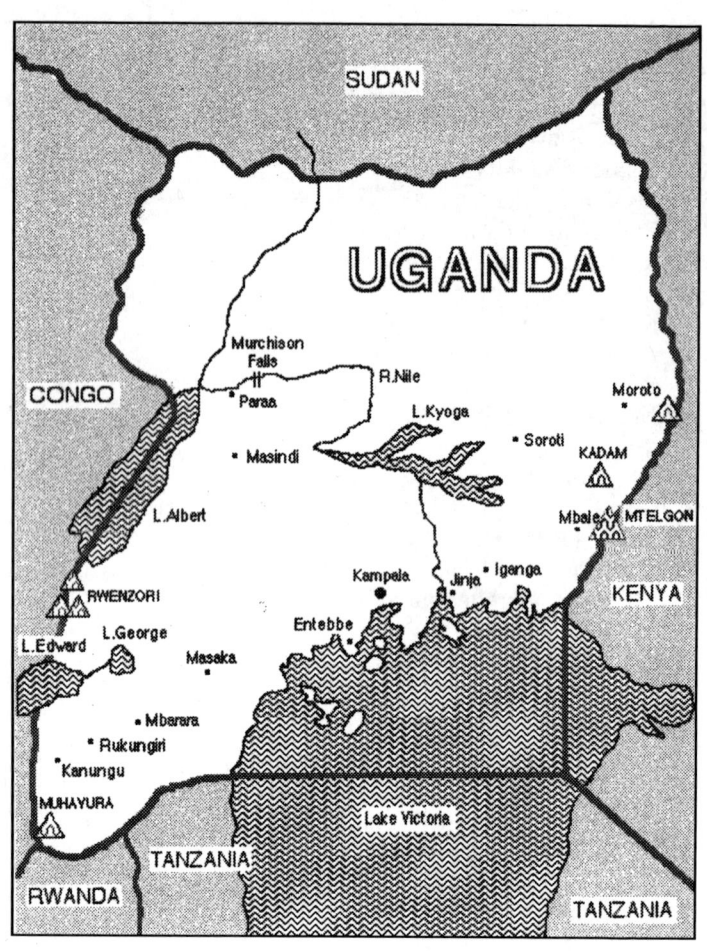

1. WHY UGANDA?

Uganda, once called 'the pearl of Africa', is still a very beautiful country. Although directly on the equator it is high enough above sea level to have a pleasant summer climate. The mountains and hills of the fertile south-west contrast sharply with the arid flat lands of the north and east, dotted with extinct volcanoes and inselbergs giving views up to a hundred miles. To the south lies Lake Victoria, vast like the sea, with islands and sandy beaches, while in the west the mighty Rwenzori range hides its snowy head and fabulous vegetation in cloud most of the time. I had experienced all this when I first lived in Uganda in the 1960s and again at intervals from 1987-1994 on a mountaineering expedition and two visits with Girl Guide groups, but it was not to revisit these wonderful places or recapture the adventures of youth that I returned to Uganda in 1997. I wanted to do something useful and help in the reconstruction of the country I loved. It had already made enormous progress since its devastation during the disastrous period of dictatorships and war in the 1970s and '80s. Besides I longed, for a change, to have just one job to which I could devote all my time and energy, after many years of carefully juggling the demands of five children, a husband who was abroad for three months of every year, a large house and garden, some secondary school teaching and voluntary work. After my husband's retirement, our youngest daughter's final year at university and the imminent end of my teaching career, my full-time return to voluntary work, preferably in Uganda, became a real possibility.

Applications to various Non-Governmental Organisations bore little fruit, until I was sent to Madagascar by BESO to help secondary teachers near the capital with their English. This experience made me realise that achieving anything worthwhile in education in such a short time is impossible. VSO (Voluntary Service Overseas) to whom I had earlier applied for another job and who normally expected a two year commitment, had no secondary teaching jobs in Uganda. Running out of possibilities,

I did a TEFL (Teaching English as a Foreign Language) Diploma by correspondence course. Then, at a VSO open day for teachers, an advertisement for teacher trainers in Uganda caught my eye. I discovered that I was adequately qualified and applied.

Three months later I found myself in a teacher training college off the beaten track in eastern Uganda, an area of rolling farmland and trees, interspersed with swamps, many converted into rice fields. My threefold assignment committed me to teaching in the English department, assisting with the organisation of teaching practice and involvement in the training of the college tutors. Three or four two-hour lectures a week constituted a full teaching timetable to classes of between nine and twenty three students with 'A' level English training to teach in secondary schools. During their holidays, which coincided with school holidays, about seven hundred experienced primary teachers descended on the college, working for a higher qualification at their own expense. They had to take either English or mathematics as one of their subjects and two thirds always chose English, giving us classes of over a hundred with a wide age and ability range. It took a while to get used to the enormous classes and the long teaching sessions, but I enjoyed the classroom work. The small groups of young secondary teachers were rewarding in their frank and often appreciative response, while the primary teachers were very keen and anxious to do well, although personal contact with more than a few proved difficult. The self-imposed challenge of marking at least one piece of written work from each of them in every one of the short terms they spent with us kept me very busy even during their absence.

My main reason for wanting to return to Uganda was that I felt I would be more useful in a country I already knew. It did indeed make an enormous difference, I think, as familiarity with the people's history and ways facilitated a quicker, easier and perhaps more intimate contact with them. Living in an unfamiliar part of the country and under very different conditions from any I had previously experienced was unexpectedly challenging and exciting. The middle-class Ugandan society in which I found myself had surprising similarities with the hopes and aspirations of such people at home, in spite of great differences in their circumstances. The picture of Africans as abjectly poor victims of starvation and disease so prevalent in the developed world, and the African perception of whites as the wealthy distributors of endless bounty from the vast resources of the first world both proved misleading. While I saw myself as richer than the people whose stories are told here, other local people were far better off than I was. I tried not to be an easy touch for anyone who took the trouble to beg – and plenty of people did. Nearly all the characters I helped wanted to do something for themselves to improve their situation rather than just receive hand-outs for further study.

Injustice and corruption always seemed to target the most deprived, who rarely complained. This was difficult to live with. Poverty is a complicated concept, often seen merely as the absence of material goods. But naked Ugandan toddlers are not necessarily the children of destitute parents: they wear nothing because it is hot and they get dirty in a country where water for washing clothes means extra work. For all their lack of worldly goods – or perhaps because of it – these people were more cheerful, friendly and open to others than their wealthy counterparts. They loved and enjoyed celebrations and feasts with a fervour which those who never go without things simply can not emulate. Their unfailing hospitality put ours to shame. We have much to learn from them with regard to interpersonal relationships and the cheerful acceptance of life as it comes.

As I did not wish to bore the reader with a diary of the experiences of two and a half years which do not make a coherent narrative, I have settled for a kaleidoscope of people's stories, events and topics, which overlap in time. Names have been changed but everything else is authentic. The sketches which follow are chiefly intended to entertain, but I hope that they will also lead to an appreciation of the challenges facing the middle classes in a rapidly changing Africa, and raise awareness and create a better understanding of this huge and largely ignored part of the world community.

Typical road with Muvule tree in rural Busoga (see p.159)

2. THE MONEY TREE

Pale of skin I may well be,
And come from far across the sea,
So that you think you get from me
A scholarship or student fee;
A visit to a far country;
A bicycle; a piggery:
Whate'er your hearts desire might be.
I'd love to give it to you free,
But I am not a money tree:
Cash doesn't simply grow on me.
I have to work to earn my fee,
So don't expect too much of me.
I only wish that you would see,
However much I'd like to be,
I am just NOT a money tree.

I had travelled to Uganda in a group of twelve VSO volunteers, three of them like me destined to work in National Teachers Colleges, the rest in a variety of other projects and places, mostly in the west. We had spent nearly three weeks in Kampala on in-country training and language lessons before being released to our employers. The four college staff among us were carried off to the annual conference for tutor training at Masindi before the end of our three weeks and so it came about that Marjorie, a volunteer who had worked in Uganda for many years, rather than someone from the VSO office or the college, took me to my new home. As we travelled east beyond Jinja the hills grew lower and the countryside more parched – and my heart sank. I had hoped to buy fruit and vegetables at a roadside stall on the way, but there were none. The area had in fact suffered an unexpected drought and looked uncharacteristically brown, dusty and desolate, with fields of dry maize stalks reaching forlornly into the pale sky. Even Marjorie was a little shocked that only some very small tomatoes and desiccated little bananas were on offer at a large stall outside the town, before we drove down a track to the college so rough that her Suzuki could only just cope with it.

Marjorie knew the college and, having seen my house, had prepared me for something pretty bad. The college seemed deserted when we arrived but eventually we found the man with the key to my house. Marjorie was amazed at the change that a coat of cream paint instead of the former dirty blue had made to its appearance. It certainly looked more attractive than she had led me to expect.

Marjorie had to leave almost at once to return to her college before sunset, as we were discouraged from being on the road after dark. As the Suzuki disappeared between the neat green hedges so did the last white person I was to see for two weeks. I went into the house destined to be my home for the next two and a half years. Living alone in this remote spot where I knew no one would be strange after many years in a family home, but not an entirely new experience.

The house, designed along with the rest of the college by an American architect some twenty years earlier and uncared for since, felt like a goldfish bowl, with glass walls at both ends of the large living room. Some big broken panes had been replaced by wooden planks or metal sheets, but a good deal of window remained, inadequately covered by limp pieces of faded pink material. The door leading to the road was solid wood with a lock and key, the one at the garden end was very wide, half glazed and had to be bolted from inside. I kept both wide open whenever I was in to catch the slightest breeze. The high sloping ceiling covered with rush matting to cut down the heat from the asbestos roof above turned out to be a fine home for ants, lizards and possibly rats.

There was no time to consider the surroundings or the people gazing in from a safe distance. Aware that the electricity was likely to be off from seven until eleven, as it was on alternate evenings throughout the country, I had to get something to eat and make the bed, preferably fixing the mosquito net as well. A large cardboard box contained everything I was supposed to need apart from basic furniture and my personal luggage. Unpacking the box felt like Christmas: new sheets and blankets, a double electric hotplate, a mini paraffin cooker, hurricane lamps, pots and pans and two twenty-litre jerry cans. Despite having no running water, the house boasted a bathroom with bath and flush toilet, only the basin was missing – cut off at the wall.

Darkness fell quickly at about seven like every night of the year. The electricity stayed on this time. The kitchen light turned on normally. The security lights outside functioned, but could I get the lights to work in the big room? I rushed from the double switches beside one door to those at the other trying various combinations before both ceiling lights suddenly lit up together. It took me days to work out that they always had to be switched on where they had been turned off, and that the bathroom light did not work if the main lights or either of the security lights were on. Amazing wiring! After dark it was most unusual for anyone to come to the door, and that first night I was undisturbed.

Dawn came as swiftly as the night at about seven, heralded by cockerels and other birds, soon followed by the bleating of goats, the creaking of pit latrine doors at the end of our gardens and people setting out to work in the fields. In the cool clear air the sun rose into a red and gold sky shading to deep blue overhead. It remained fresh until about nine. I managed to light the paraffin stove and put the kettle on for a much needed cup of coffee.

Two jerry cans full of water had been left in the house. Mr. Musuki, the estates officer who had checked me in, said I could leave them at the roadside to be refilled every morning when the tractor came for the director's water. Now an endless procession of people in tattered clothes passed along the road at the front of the house to fetch water from the borehole. The men and big boys usually rode bicycles; the women and children carried the bright yellow or green jerry cans on their heads, the younger children using smaller cans, right down to the toddlers, who barely managed to keep up. In addition to the cans on their heads most of the women had babies tied on their backs.

Soon the procession changed to children in neat clean turquoise dresses or shirts on their way to school. Some of these ventured near the house when they noticed the open door to have a look at the new *muzungu*. In fact, children peered round the strange walls outside at all hours of the day, and probably the night, for the next few weeks. I was a great source of interest and entertainment in the absence of other excitement.

My house stood at the end of a terrace of four. Free-standing walls, painted light yellow like the outside of the house, some with built-in holes, provided a little privacy, acting as hedges between the homes. The ground in front of the big window was scraped bare, as was a much larger area behind the house. The latter had a strange mound in the centre where, I later learned, one of my predecessors had built a hut for sitting out in the cool of evening. Not a stick remained. On the detached side the blank wall was bordered by a wide path and a large grassy open space up to a hedge and a dirt road.

Soon Mr Musuki called for me. Officially he was the estates officer, but he did much else besides. He invited me to ride on the back of his bicycle to the main college buildings, about five minutes walk away, to meet the director and such members of staff as were around. As we rode along the paths between neat bright green hedges of yellow-flowering milkweed, past the small nursery school building, curious mounds showed through the dry brown grass on our right. These foundations for further buildings had been excavated in the mid-seventies, but abandoned when Uganda sank into chaos and the contractor ran off with the money. The lecture rooms looked similarly abandoned with sheets of plasterboard and electric wires hanging from the ceilings, doors missing, window panes gone and little paint left on the walls. In a series of small offices in a better state of repair, I was welcomed by cheerful friendly people. After meeting the director and the administrative staff, the five members the English department gathered in its little storeroom-like office. Two tables, three chairs and some shelving and a cupboard on one wall constituted the furniture, while a high window let in some light and two wooden shutters fresh air when they were unbolted. The shelves were crammed with books, including some new and very useful ones, mostly donated by the British Council. More chairs for us had to be found in similar offices, where everything was kept carefully locked up. The meeting went well. I was asked what I would like to teach, and opted for language rather than literature which turned out to be a wise and popular move. I shared this section of the syllabus with Christopher, a former head of the department, who had taught it for many years. We got on very well together, not least because we both felt frustrated by the present head, who only appeared on two mornings a week, showed little interest in our work but worried about others taking over his job.

Term should have started the previous week but very few students had put in an appearance. They began to collect their fees from their relations only on the day they were supposed to start college and it could take a long time before they managed to gather enough. The extended family was usually expected to contribute to young people's training, placing an enormous burden on those who were earning well and encouraging them to have large families of their own, because otherwise they had to pay for their younger siblings, nephews and nieces.

Walking back to my house after the meeting I came across small groups of cheerful, smiling children, the girls invariably sinking to their knees, as they said 'Good morning, Madam.' The little boys were not always quite so polite and I was quite shocked when one or two of them followed up the greeting with a bold 'Give me my money!'

'Your money? I haven't got your money! Why are you asking me?' soon saw them off in fits of giggles. They must have been the children of college staff to be so bold and know so much English. I wondered what their parents would have thought of this behaviour, but soon learnt that it would not have surprised them in the least. Using the imperative *give* was not rude but a direct translation from the vernacular, which has no word for *please*.

Shortly after I got home there was a knock on the back door. A young man in clean shirt and trousers stood outside.

'Good morning, Madam. How are you, Madam? How was the night? How's here?'

I answered politely, wondering about the purpose of the visit. I didn't have to wait long.

'Can you help me, Madam?'

'That depends. Come in a minute. What do you want?'

Shoes were slipped off and the young person came in, sat down and rapidly took stock of my possessions. Disappointingly there wasn't much to see except books and papers.

'Madam, I have no money to pay my fees.'

'I am very sorry to hear that, but I don't think I can help you. I don't know who you are or anything about you. I am working as a volunteer and get no more – probably less – pay than other members of staff here. Have you asked them? I also have children at home and we are still paying fees for one at university. I can't help everybody here. Why should I choose you?'

'I have to go and see my uncle who lives far away to see if he can help me, but I haven't got the fare.'

'I am very sorry, but I really can't help you, and I must get on with my work now.'

'But, Madam.....'

'Money doesn't grow on trees, does it? Well, I'm not a money tree, so I'm sorry, I can't give you any.'

This scene was played over and over again with different people, but always the same kind of request. It was not easy and seemed churlish to deal with these poor youngsters like this, but what else could I do? In time these visits became fewer, as money was very rarely forthcoming, but it was a real relief to hear a different story as sometimes happened.

In for a penny, in for a pound;
It's love that makes the world go round.

The words of this song often went through my head, but increasingly it seemed that it isn't love but pennies and pounds that make the world go round these days, even in this remote corner. Everything revolved around money.

The currency exchange rate during my stay in Uganda ranged from 1,700/- to 2,400/- Uganda Shillings to the English pound. All the money came in notes from 10,000/- down to the almost worthless and usually creased and grubby 50/-, until the introduction of coins up to 500/- shortly before I left. Virtually all financial transactions were in cash and the amounts always sounded huge. Robbery and theft occurred frequently, so it was unwise to carry large sums. I have never borrowed as much as I did in my first few months in Uganda because I always left myself short of cash. There was no reliable method of sending money either, although the Post Office did eventually establish a proper registered mail, which was more or less theft proof. The normal method of payment was cash in person, even when considerable sums were involved. The cloak and dagger scene in which my car was purchased was a good example. The money came from England and I collected it from the headquarters of my bank in Kampala. Several million shillings meant bulky bundles of notes. As instructed I put them in my rucksack in the private office at the back where I received them, away from prying eyes, before going out to meet the friend who had arranged the car deal.

'We must take a taxi,' he said.

Settled in the back, he asked me to put the money surreptitiously into his briefcase.

At the dealer's, an insignificant spares shop, my car was parked at the kerb. We went inside and my friend disappeared behind the counter with the cash. In utmost secrecy under the counter he counted the money out to the dealer. When an employee came in for a spare part off the shelf, the operation was pushed out of sight. The counting took ages even when the dealer joined in, but eventually all was settled and we drove off in my little Toyota Starlet.

Banks created problems, too, including the bank we volunteers were encouraged to sign up with because it used electronic transfer to move our allowances to our accounts in a few days, unlike cheques, which took six weeks to clear. One day, just before the beginning of a school term, I went to get money from my branch in Iganga. I had a student with me and when I told her where I was going she said:

'But the bank is closed.'

'Why? It's Wednesday. Why should the bank be closed?'

'It was on the radio last night. All the banks of that group were closed by the government.'

Sure enough, when we arrived, the usual armed guard was outside together with a policeman and a notice to say that the bank was closed until further notice. Not for the first time had this happened to a banking company in recent months. Return of depositors' money was immediately promised but it was many months before it was actually paid. In the meantime numerous businesses and private schools failed because their delicate cash flow received a fatal blow. Fraud and theft by bank staff caused these closures, so no one had much faith in banks as institutions. This in turn meant that people held on to large cash sums, giving rise to more robbery. The college did not fall into this trap. They insisted that all fees were paid into the bank – twenty miles away. It was also a good excuse for not paying staff on time: the bursar had no time to go to the bank or there was no transport. The best excuse he ever gave me was 'The bank had no money'. Colleagues assured me that even this could be true.

3. THE CHILDREN

The nursery school was on my way to college. As soon as the children spotted me when I passed in mid-morning squeals of delight were followed by cries of '*Muzungu!*' as about a dozen cheerful three and four year-olds came rushing through the hedge to shake hands. The beautifully dressed little girls always sank to their knees as all females, even old ladies, were expected to do whenever they greeted anybody. A few children hung back, not brave enough to shake a white hand, while the bold ones ran to the end of the line to do it again, always accompanied by, 'Good morning, *Muzungu.*'

Muzungu, the generic for a white person, was often shouted in great excitement when one was spotted in an unexpected place. Occasionally someone asked if I found it insulting, which I did not, but it seemed inappropriate from these children as time went on. One day I mentioned it to their teacher and suggested they use whatever name or title she thought suitable. After that I was 'Madam'. When a school child called me '*Muzungu*' I addressed it '*Musoga*', the word for an individual of the local tribe. I am not sure that they even noticed.

Many pupils passed my house on their way to the Demonstration or Dem School, formerly used as such when the college had trained only primary teachers. Some of the older children, especially girls, began to visit in groups of three or four. One of them, usually a lecturer's child, could speak reasonable English while the rest just sat, having a good look round. They probably thought me inhospitable, as I did not offer them anything to eat or drink in the customary way, but I had nothing suitable and only four glasses – even when the washing up was done. It was difficult to remember who was who and whether they had called before, so that I didn't ask them all the same questions again. Language difficulties hampered conversation. Though they had learned English for some years, the children were far from fluent in speaking and had problems understanding my accent, but we usually managed to establish ages, family size and where they lived. They sometimes asked for books or penfriends, and one or two successful exchanges of letters came about.

One group of girls came quite often, especially while my son was visiting. They loved talking to him and he was very patient with them. Their spokeswoman was Sara, a small, neat, self-possessed child, the daughter of the Dem School headmaster. Her English was good enough to give a graphic account of life in the classroom with the *'boda-boda* boys', the young men who provided bicycle transport.

'They sit at the back of the class and make a noise. They talk and make jokes about the teacher. They do whatever they like and it upsets the teachers.'

'Why don't the teachers throw them out?'

'The boys say they are also people's children, so they are entitled to free education now – but they are bad.'

Fortunately these 'boys' did not last long in the classroom, but they added to the general chaos for a while.

Sara was soon sent to one of the country's best boarding schools, but she continued to visit me during her holidays and even wrote occasionally. When her family moved from the campus she asked if she could come and stay. Thinking she would spend most of her time with her old friends, I readily agreed. One Sunday evening at the beginning of the Christmas holidays Sara turned up to stay without further warning. Fortunately I had been expecting a friend who had not come, so the bed was made and there was enough to eat. The first evening passed pleasantly enough, but next morning Sara seemed to want to stay in the house while I went out to teach. I was not keen to have a crowd of girls investigating every nook and cranny in my absence. Besides, there was only one key and I did not like to leave the house unlocked with no-one in if Sara went out, so I asked her to visit her friends as long as I was out.

The atmosphere became slightly strained and I felt that something was amiss, but had no idea what it might be. When I had to go to Iganga next day, she told me she would like to come and then go home the following day.

On the way back from Iganga she suddenly said without looking at me, 'Dad wonders if you can sponsor me – or find someone else who can.'

'What do you mean? Sponsor you for what?'

'Well... pay my school fees and help me with other things.'

'How many brothers and sisters have you got?'

'Three.'

'Do you know how many people ask me to sponsor them? Most of them need it much more than you. You have a mother and a father with a very well-paid job. Why do you need a sponsor, when there are so many orphans and children of poor parents? I am sorry but I don't think you need help.'

I got the impression that her father had sent her purely to make this request, which embarrassed her. She hardly spoke to me again. She stayed out until bedtime when we got back, left early the next morning and I never heard from her again. When I met her father months later he was cheerful enough. There was clearly no ill-feeling on his part.

The children came during their holidays, which were not holidays for me. In time their visits became fewer as the novelty wore off, I was out more often or had students in. One day a young man came on a bicycle. His name was Robert and when I asked him about his school, I was surprised to learn that he was still at the primary school, for which he seemed a little old. He wondered if I could help him. It was not quite the usual story of no father and dozens of siblings. He did have lots of brothers and sisters, but he wanted to do something useful to help his family. Could I help him set up a money-raising project? This sounded splendid: Robert actually wanted to do something himself.

'What kind of project are you thinking of?' I asked him.

'I could maybe start trading,' he answered.

'Have you anything to sell?'

'Well, no; not really. You can buy some things for me to sell.'

I didn't approve of this idea, but Robert was not put off so easily.

'What I would really like to do is start a pig project,' he said.

'And have you anywhere to keep pigs?'

'We have room at home. Can you get some piglets for me?'

'Do you know anything about keeping pigs? It's not so easy: they need proper feeding and care. Can you manage that?' I wanted to know.

'Well, I don't know, but my sister knows. She had pigs.'

'Excellent. Then why don't you ask your sister to give you a piglet to start off with?'

'She hasn't got them now.'

'Why not?'

'They're all dead.'

'Oh. So it seems that keeping pigs is not so easy after all. I think you had better go away and think of something you really can do.'

Still not deterred, Robert changed tack again and asked if I would consider taking him to Jinja. He had never been to the big town. He had never been anywhere in a car. I agreed to take him to Iganga if I was going straight there and back, which sometimes happened, but usually I went further and stayed away over night. He came round a few more times to make plans, but sadly his outing never worked out.

Few boys came to visit, but one lunchtime three quite small ones loitered around my front door on their way home from school. When asked what they wanted, they managed with some difficulty to say that they had only come to greet me. So we greeted each other very formally.

After a pause one of them said:

'We are hungry. Give us something to eat.'

'Are you not going home? Will you not get food at home? I'm very sorry, but I can't feed you. If I give you something today, then tomorrow all the other children who go home this way will want the same. That's impossible!'

It is unlikely that they actually understood what I said, but they got the message and slowly disappeared down the road.

Other children I knew only by reputation, such as Emma. Across the road they were always shouting for or at Emma. This was surprising because girls on the whole were quiet and kept busy indoors with domestic chores. Emma clearly roamed – and misbehaved. When I inquired who Emma was everyone laughed at me. Emma was not one but two little boys! Two families across the road had sons called Emmanuel, both quite naughty ten-year-olds who played together and were often in trouble. There were no female Emmas anywhere.

Another name that I kept hearing for a while was Elena. She clearly was a girl who lived next door. One of her friends used to stand in the road and screech monotonously for ten minutes at a time 'Eeleenaa!' I have no idea why she did not come up to the house, unless she was afraid of me next door. I was never quite sure exactly who some of these children were, but Elena, a pretty child with laughing eyes, stood out because she was rather naughty, *stubborn* as my neighbours would say. At the back of the house I had sown flower seeds and eventually three plants grew pretty purple blooms. Once I came back after a weekend away to find them gone. At first I suspected goats, but closer inspection revealed holes that looked as though the plants had been dug up. It was not the first time that things had disappeared from my garden, but it was more than a little surprising to see my flowers in the otherwise bare nextdoor front yard a few days later. What to do? I didn't want unpleasantness with the neighbours but I did want my flowers back. I checked with friends that it would not be offensive to ask about them before finally plucking up the courage to go next door.

'Oh, I had no idea they came from your garden,' said my neighbour. 'Elena brought them and planted them here.'

'Do you mind if I take them back? I would like them to seed and then Elena can have some of the seedlings. She can have some of my marigolds now if she is keen to grow flowers.'

But Elena was not that keen.

Boys at play

Watching the children play was a delight – most of the time. The boys played football with a ball made of polythene bags tied with string. This was said to be better than banana fibre, though not as attractive, but a good use for the refuse which otherwise defaced the compound. Sometimes the young lads rushed through the garden in posses in pursuit of whatever was in season: ants or grasshoppers; or they mercilessly stoned the big mango trees before the fruit was ripe – a noisy, dangerous and most annoying pastime. The younger boys ran after the older ones or just stood and watched them, trying to imitate what they were doing. It was lovely to see how much pleasure they derived from their simple games in the sunshine. Yet they were not always good. One morning I heard strange noises on the roof. They sounded heavier than the crows which often landed there, and I thought they might be ground hornbills, turkey-sized black birds with red wattles, which occasionally appeared in the fields. But these birds were human: four little neighbours' boys had climbed to the roof behind their house and then teetered their way along the parapet on the edge to the houses nextdoor.

'What do you think you are doing up there?' had them scuttling back quickly to where they had climbed a lemon tree to get to the roof.

Most children on the campus were not permanent residents, one reason which made it difficult to get to know them. Many only stayed there in term time to go to school and went back to the village for the holidays, even if their parents lived at the college. Others were relations who came just to go to school. The house next door had a complete change of inhabitants for school holidays, as my colleague to whom the house was allocated, did not actually live there. His sister, a teacher in the primary school, did. During the holidays she went back to the village and the house was let to student primary teachers with babies, as they were not allowed in the halls of residence. It started with two or three, but the numbers grew and during my last primary session, the house was occupied by no fewer than eight mothers with babies as well as the slightly older children who looked after them. The latter made a great deal of noise as they played around my house and watched my every move with fascination never having lived near a *muzungu* before. The numerous other neighbourhood children joined them. The prospect of six weeks of this was daunting. One afternoon I was marking exercises at home when one of the little girls sat on the low bank opposite my front door with a crying baby. She sat for a long time, doing nothing to comfort the child. I decided not to complain, so I went to the bedroom. The cries pursued me until I could bear it no longer.

'Go and sit somewhere else, please,' I said, waving her away. The instant she got to her feet the bored baby stopped crying.

That evening I went round to the students to suggest that they find at least one adult to keep their mob in order.

'We are sorry the children have disturbed you. We shall speak to them,' they said. 'Don't worry.'

I had no need to. It was so peaceful from then on that I went back intrigued two weeks later. The eight beds were still in the living room.

'Have some of you left? Have you sent the children home?' I asked the mother bathing her little one in a bowl at the front door.

'No, no. We are all still here,' she answered. 'We told the children not to bother you and to go and play somewhere else.'

How I wish all my suggestions had been so effectively followed!

Once a week I took my first-year secondary student teachers to the Dem school to get a little hands-on experience with the top class. The younger children, having already finished lessons, found this so interesting that they hung around the doors and windows in noisy clusters making it difficult for my students to work with their classes. Moving from room to room I felt like the Pied Piper. At other times the children appeared at the windows of my classroom in the college, which was also disturbing. They took no notice of the students when they remonstrated with them so one day we brought in a persistent offender to sit through a class. Even that deterred them only briefly. In the end I decided their headmaster would have to deal with this. When I went to see him he thought my presence was the big attraction so it might help if I met the whole school at assembly one morning. Then they could all have a good look and I would ask them publicly with unmistakable translation to stay away from our lessons. The youngest children were to get an extra treat: I would visit them in class. As a result one fine morning I greeted and briefly spoke to about a thousand children neatly lined up in the shade of their school building cast by the early morning sun, before shaking over two hundred sticky little hands amidst great excitement in Primary 1. That was not quite the end of the story: soon a rumour circulated that I was to be the new head teacher. Happily there was no chance of this happening.

4. LAMENT OF THE MANGO TREE

Dear children,
I am a big, sad mango tree.
My shade I give to you for free,
And flowers and fruits grow well on me.
Why then, when my first fruits you see,
Do you throw sticks and bricks and stones at me?
My richly laden branches break with cruelty?
What wrong could I have done that you should be
So horrid, that you treat me in this way so wickedly?
All just because you want to take away from me
The hard green little bitter mangoes that you see?
Wait until large and ripe these fruits shall be.
Then I will let them fall for you most generously.
(No need to risk a fall by climbing up the tree.)
Much better for your health too they will be
When sweet they are and more juicy.
Please, children, listen to my plea:
Just let me be!
A mango tree,
A lovely tree,
A shady tree,
A useful tree,
A fruitful tree,
For all to see
My lush beauty.
TAKE CARE OF ME!

A version of the poem was published by one of the national newspapers when I sent it in as a warning to the stone-throwing children in the mango season.

5. ELECTIONS

A number of lecture-free days occurred in my first term. I would turn up in the classroom at a quarter to eight to find everywhere deserted and the offices shut. Eventually someone would tell me that a radio announcement the night before had declared the day a public holiday. One of these occasions was for the election of the committee of the lowest tier of local government, the Local Council 1, LC1.

Uganda has a policy, highly regarded in the West, of devolving government from the centre, the President and democratically elected Parliament, closer to the people in the districts. The smallest units of local government were village councils of ten members with specific tasks in the community. At least one member had to be a woman. The pattern was repeated at higher levels, giving LCs 1 to 5, LC5 being the District or Municipal Council. Nationally the elections started at the lowest level and gradually over a period of months worked up to LC5. Voters had to register and produce their cards, although at the lowest levels they were known by everybody, so this was not always enforced. In the early stages voting took the form of *lining up;* the voters simply stood in a straight line behind their chosen candidate and were counted by the returning officer.

The college staff were sufficiently numerous for the college to have village status and an LC1 committee. On the day appointed for the election I expected great excitement, but all was quiet like a Sunday morning. Voting was due to start at ten, but only the college registrar who was responsible for the arrangements was in his office and not very happy at the general lack of interest. He advised me to go home and come back later. After two hours a handful of people had gathered outside the offices and the registrar finally decided to go ahead under the mango tree a hundred yards from the college offices which seemed to be a recognised meeting place. A desk and chair and a bench were brought and the returning officer, a shy young lady teacher from the primary school who was also one of our students, was summoned. About a dozen people, mostly staff members, had gathered under the tree by the time she arrived with her exercise book to register the voters. Considerable discussion followed, partly in Lusoga, the local language, which I could not follow, as a result of which they decided to allow me to register as well as two members of staff who had sent a message with a friend to register them. More voters were awaited, but none came. In the end it was decided to proceed with those present, who included four women. One of these, an articulate secondary school teacher and wife of a lecturer, wanted to stand for chairman. This was very progressive, as some of the lecturers would not even let their wives vote – voting was men's business, they claimed. After more delays and no further arrivals it was agreed that enough people to form the committee were present. The chairman and secretary would be elected from among them and the remaining posts would be shared out. The two candidates for chairman were sent out of hearing range, while their proposers made speeches about their suitability. When they returned we lined up behind the candidate of our choice to be counted. The lady won by one vote, but this was quickly overturned by the men claiming that the two registered voters who were still absent intended to vote for the male candidate, so he was declared the winner, the lady becoming vice-chairman. I thought this most unjust – and said so. Finally all the vacancies were filled except that of women's representative. A number of names were proposed before considerable pressure was brought to bear on one of the ladies present, who seemed eminently suitable for this post but persisted in her refusal to fill it. This was Ruth – more about her later. When I got to know her better I came to understand her reasons.

From the number of people I saw queuing later in the day on my way to Iganga, this was clearly not a typical response to the opportunity to elect political leaders. The college was not really a village community as it had a natural head in the director and the senior staff were already responsible for dealing with the matters which concerned LC1s, such as discipline, hygiene and services within the community.

The next stage of the election for LC2 and LC3 councillors I witnessed in Kampala at Nsambya hospital, the nearest polling station to the home of an old friend where I was a frequent visitor. This time colourful posters described the election procedure in pictures and Luganda, but the *lining up* procedure was still followed. Again it took time to gather the voters, most in this case being the nurses, who came from all over the country. Many had to be sent back to their rooms for their voting cards, while those who had none could not vote. Eventually all was ready and the voters present lined up behind their candidates, though some seemed uncertain whom to back and kept changing lines. It seemed that they just did not want the line of the losing candidate to be too short. The LC3 candidates were not actually present, so their pictures elevated on poles served instead. This time the winner had a much longer line than his opponent. The gatherings for these elections were sociable occasions with much chat and laughter; any attempts to sway opinion were calm and good-natured.

LC4 and LC5 committees were elected by secret ballot and for various reasons the election was postponed several times. Canvassing this time was wide-spread and noisy and I believe very costly for the candidates. A friend from Iganga who was standing in another district lost considerable weight during the election fight. One day he told me that he nearly starved during the campaign because when he was with people they expected him to pay for any refreshments, as he could pay himself back once they had elected him. As he was not rich and the election outcome uncertain, he simply went without meals. This does throw some light on the common attitude to corruption and particularly the theft of public money which often surprised me: it was wrong and the perpetrators should be punished, but no one ever mentioned restitution. A small-time thief in the market could be killed on the spot, but embezzling politicians had somehow earned their ill-gotten wealth.

Possibly the most corrupting influences on life in Uganda were nepotism and, closely related to it, tribalism. A person's duty was to benefit family, clan and tribe in that order. A well-paid administrator in the college asked me for a huge loan to bail his son out of police custody when he had been caught red-handed stealing from the students. As a good father he was expected to protect his son. As a good father he would also be expected to further his son's career by what ever means he could – fair or foul. In this way a number of incompetent people had attained high office, because they had wealthy families who could buy them qualifications and positions of power. The tribal issue was more or less an extension of this and in many ways very understandable. The good side of the system was that family ties remained strong, creating stability in the sense that everybody belonged to a caring group.

6. THE FEAST OF ST. MATTHIAS KALEMBA

There was no public holiday for the celebrations for the feast of St. Matthias Kalemba in the saint's home village. He was one of the Uganda martyrs killed by Kabaka Mwanga for their Christian beliefs in 1886. Mr. Musuki, the college estates officer and a man of many functions, asked if I would like to join the group going from the college. I accepted with pleasure. Departure was set for six o'clock on Sunday morning. Such arrangements were apt to be arbitrary, but it was impressed on me that an early start was essential.

On the morning in question a tremendous storm had broken in the early hours and at six the rain was streaming down in utter darkness. I knew that nothing would happen in this weather, so I took my time and only paddled to the other side of the campus when the rain eased off at about seven thirty. Although it was light by this time not a soul was about. The pick-up, covered in a blue tarpaulin, stood ready and waiting outside the Musukis' home, but with no sign of passengers. Mr Musuki, clad only in a towel, emerged from his front door and told me to sit in the pick-up, with a cheery:

'We'll be leaving soon.'

The rain dripping off the tarpaulin was the only movement for the next hour.

We did eventually leave with quite a crowd on the back. Even though the rain had stopped, various people who had agreed to come had not appeared, so Mr. Musuki drove round the campus looking for them before we finally hit the road. In the distinctly cool and damp atmosphere the poor souls on the back must have been frozen in their thin summer clothing.

We made good progress until a short round policewoman traffic officer stopped us on the highway at Iganga. She declared the vehicle unroadworthy and only after much pleading by Mr. Muzuki did she allow us to proceed. As the rain had been so heavy, we took a long way round by a better road, for even Mr.

Musuki had his doubts about the pick-up's performance in deep mud.

Brilliant sunshine made everything look fresh and gleaming by the time we reached our destination at about ten. Other worshippers had also been delayed by the rain and were just arriving. A chapel, in a hollow in the extensive grounds, was the saint's shrine, but such crowds were expected for this festive occasion that an altar had been erected outside under a shelter of tarpaulins. Everything was decorated with flowers and festooned with glittering Christmas decorations. Under further tarpaulins a large blue-robed choir began to practise. Every patch of shade under the trees was already filled with folk in their brightly coloured best clothes. There were school children like Easter eggs in their various uniforms and groups of priests and nuns in their different habits. We joined the latter on wooden benches on the wide verandah of the chapel. More and more people kept arriving. The whole area was a rainbow of humanity with gaudy umbrellas put up as sunshades adding to the colour. By the time the service started with harmonised hymns accompanied by throbbing drums, no grass was left in sight. There was, however, plenty of movement, with processions and dancing as well as the singing forming part of the service, and the crowd shifting and growing along the edges. In front of the altar clusters of small children were kept in check by an old man in a long white robe carrying a stick. As he moved them back on one side, they would drift forward again on the other, keeping him constantly on the move. Young men climbed into the surrounding jacaranda trees to see better. It was a truly biblical scene.

The colourful celebration included a long sermon, dances to bring forward the book for the gospel reading and the gifts of fruit as well as money at the offertory, endless communions distributed by a dozen priests and finally the individual introductions of all thirty or so clergy present, with each one cheered and applauded in turn. After two hours it ended and the crowds began to disperse through the grounds. At small roadside stalls an odd assortment of items was for sale: snacks, including a sour fruit I never saw anywhere else, baskets, mats, boiled eggs, soft drinks and religious books. An exhibition and recruitment drive for religious orders tried to attract customers under spreading acacia trees. Large family groups picnicked in the shade. We wandered about chatting to people, while our fellow passengers greeted family and friends. Back at the pick-up eventually, with everybody gathered ready to go, the driver's door refused to shut. After some hard bangs, it was obvious that there was a serious problem, so Mr Musuki told the man sitting between him and me to hold on to the door with his arm round the driver's back. In this way we returned to Iganga on the shorter route as the road had dried out quite well. When we arrived there, Mr Musuki got out.

'I've got some business here. I'm not coming back with you. Isa will drive you. You must tell him to go slow and be careful. He drives a bit fast,' he said to me. My heart sank.

Isa started off moderately enough, trying to hold the door shut with his elbow, but when he reached the good straight road beyond the town, he began to pick up speed.

'You are going too fast,' I said, as the speed governor bell began to chime.

Isa slowed down – but not for long.

'Don't go so fast,' I urged again. 'Let me hold the door, so you can at least keep both hands on the wheel.'

He slowed down while I passed my arm round his back and grasped the door. That felt marginally safer, but Isa could not resist increasing his speed on this road.

'Slow down!' I warned every few minutes until we turned off on the rutted track to the college. Here Isa did slow down, but hanging on to the door needed all my concentration. Great was my relief when we reached the college safely and I could take my arm from behind his back. The saint must have been watching over us.

7. PAUL'S BICYCLE

Everybody who was anybody in our area had a bicycle. Driving back alone in the cool of evening I often counted over five hundred of them on and beside the twenty miles of good tarmac road from Iganga to the college. In the trading centres there were more than I could count in passing, as all the *boda-bodas* were waiting to take mini-bus passengers from the trading centres to remoter places. At least a dozen of these bicycle taxis with their bright red padded carriers stood at the turning to the teachers college, too. Most cyclists were men, but occasionally one saw a woman in a long, flowing *busuti* riding along with baby on back, or a boy, too small to get over the crossbar, pedalling crab-wise underneath it. Everything and everybody, alive or dead, was carried on bicycles: mountainous sacks of charcoal, chickens, goats, huge bunches of green bananas, great bubbles of cabbages or pineapples, drinks crates, jerry cans full of water, paraffin or *malwa*, the local brew, furniture, especially beds, and even coffins, occupied as well as empty. Hundreds of bicycles parked outside secondary schools were ridden home with one, two or even more passengers.

Paul lived across the road from me with his mother Ruth and seven siblings. His father, a lecturer at the college, had died in a bizarre bicycle accident earlier that year, making Paul an orphan by local reckoning. Someone had suggested that he might like to fetch my water, as the piped water system in the houses had long ceased to work and all water had to be hand pumped from a borehole about five minutes walk away. As everybody went there and it took time to fill each jerry can, the borehole was a great centre of entertainment and gossip, especially in the coolness of the morning and at sunset.

A slim, smiling twelve-year-old, Paul came with his mother the first time to settle the details of his job as his English was not very good. He did not look strong enough to carry a full twenty litre jerry can, but he was tough and had probably been doing it for his family for some time. He was to come after school every day and fill the two cans I left in front of the house. For this he would be paid the normal rate of a hundred shillings per can. Any changes of plan were to be given to him in writing to avoid any misunderstandings.

'What are you going to do with the money you earn, Paul?' I asked.

'Buy a bicycle.'

'You will have to save a very long time for that.' A bike cost about ninety thousand shillings.

'Yes,' he replied firmly.

His mother explained that he could use the bicycle to go to school as well as for fetching the water two jerry cans at a time, instead of one on his head. The family already owned a bicycle but the demands on it were great, as three or four of them needed it regularly.

'What a good idea. I'll help you save your money. We'll keep the record of what you earn on a card and you can watch it grow. When you have saved a reasonable amount we'll open a savings account for you.'

It seemed a good idea to teach Paul and his family about saving and getting interest, but implementing it was not possible, as the banks did not give accounts to children before they had an identity card, which they could not have until they were fourteen. So every month I put Paul's money in an envelope in my safe. He could boost his earnings further by doing odd jobs in the garden and washing the car, his favourite activity. He proudly shared this privileged task with his friends, who liked to have a look and fiddle about inside the car. They always did a good job with very little water and would happily have done it every day, though it was a complete waste of time, as the car was covered in dust or mud depending on the weather before it even reached the tarmac road.

After a few weeks Paul brought a thousand shillings he had saved at home to put with his earnings. I was impressed, but not yet ready to buy the bicycle until I was quite sure I could trust him to go on working for me once he had it. He carried out his duties faithfully for about six months. The family had to move in with relations nearby when his mother lost her job as one of the college nurses and their staff house. This meant that he had a little further to come. Finally, before I went on leave for a month I decided the time had come to buy the bicycle. Paul could perhaps use it to earn a little money during the school holidays and my absence by helping someone else.

I asked him to find out precisely what he wanted and how much it would cost, but this led to a communications failure, so we asked my colleague David to help as he lived near the bicycle shops in town. He promised to make enquiries and negotiate a fair price.

Paul on his bicycle with his brother and sister and his friend on the front

David came with us on the great day of the purchase, solving the language problem and preventing the cost from inflating for my benefit. With grave deliberation Paul and David chose a strong black basic model. Two strengthening bars had to be fitted from the handlebars to the front axle and the carrier also had to be adapted to bear extra weight. This enabled Paul to carry his friends or two jerry cans at once strapped to the carrier. He danced for joy and could hardly wait the few days before he could take his treasure home. He always treated his machine with loving care and kept it shining.

Soon Paul really needed the bike when his family moved to the next village and he had much further to go. He still turned up regularly, almost always with a friend or two on the crossbar. Bicycle ownership was good for Paul's status, while the contact with me was good for his English, which improved considerably with time.

Long before he had cleared his debt, repairs became necessary. When Paul said he needed a new tyre, I realised for the first time the full meaning of *threadbare*. That the tyre had not burst was a miracle. I bought the spares, and Paul's older brother James did the repairs and maintenance work. Such jobs were always done at the last possible moment, but they did get done. Paul regarded his bicycle as something precious, perhaps not surprisingly as he had worked very hard for it.

One day Paul invited me to his school open day. Thinking it might be quite interesting, I accepted. I hoped to go with his mother, but she had to work, so James came with me. We arrived at the school at about half past eleven. I expected to go round the class rooms, perhaps have a word with Paul's teacher, and be out half an hour later. Not in Uganda. As soon as we had gone through the gate one of the pupils conducted us to an area near the classrooms, where chairs were set out under the usual tarpaulin awning facing the stage, an area which had been levelled and swept. I was immediately taken to an armchair at the front. Not allowed to sit with me, James found a wooden chair in the row behind. Half an hour later the guest of honour, the *Kyabazinga of Busoga*, the traditional ruler of the area, was ushered in by the boys' brass band from a secondary school in the district headquarters. An elderly gentleman in a tweed suit, the *Kyabazinga* was shown to a comfortable-looking sofa right in front of the stage. He sat there alone, with his *Katikiro*, his chief secretary, in an armchair beside the sofa. Many people came to greet him, all women and children and even some men kneeling deferentially.

We sat there for the next six and a half hours, while the children performed songs, dances and recitations and sixteen adults made speeches. As the sun moved overhead, the heat became oppressive. There was no break, although it often took time for the next class to get organised on the stage. When the interval was too long the band was asked to play. No food and, worse, nothing to drink was offered. The guest of honour was given a glass of water at one point, but even he had had to ask for it. At about five o'clock the distribution of prizes to the pupils began. The prizes for various kinds of achievement were all very useful: exercise books, pencils, brightly coloured wash basins and mugs. At this point the Chief Administrative Officer, the highest central government official of the area arrived, so when the prizes had all been given out, he made another half-hour speech, repeating no doubt what the other speakers had already said. Only one speech had been in English, so I could only guess at the content of the others. The sun was sinking when we were finally free to go. An invitation to a meal was issued, but this was likely to entail another long wait. I was so desperate for a drink, that I made my excuses and left, after being introduced to the poor *Kyabazinga* who was still confined to his lonely sofa.

Paul did quite well in his primary leaving examination. The problem once again was money for him to attend secondary school. His mother must have leaned very heavily on her wealthier relations, for eventually the boy was sent to a boarding school far away. By the time the arrangements had been made, the new school year had long started, but it was quite normal for students in all institutions to turn up late. Worse was that they were not allowed to sit for exams in the second and third terms until they had paid all their fees. Often at those times one found quite small classes because so many children had been sent home. I only hope this will not happen to Paul. His job and his bicycle passed to his younger brother Michael. By this time Paul had grown considerably in stature and maturity. The only thing that remained unchanged was his smile.

8. RACHEL'S STUDENT DAYS

One day soon after my arrival and before many students were about, a well-built young woman in a brown flowered dress and with straightened hair knocked on the back door. I was prepared for the usual request for financial assistance and was delighted when after the lengthy greeting Rachel introduced herself and explained that she was a student and just wanted to know how I was getting on. When I invited her in, she took off her shoes, made herself comfortable in an armchair and accepted a cup of tea and a biscuit.

Rachel was not studying English, so I would not be teaching her. She was in her second and final year of History and Religious Studies. These subjects were very popular as they were supposed to be easy at 'A'Level, so the college classes were huge and job prospects afterwards correspondingly poor. In contrast few students qualified for English so the classes were very small. The same was true of maths, physics, chemistry, even agriculture, art and business studies, not to mention music which had more staff than students and was not a school subject.

Rachel's family lived nearby on the edge of the campus. Her father lectured in Religious Studies, as well as running a parish somewhere. Her mother had recently been made redundant by the college along with a number of other ancillary staff. In spite of this, Rachel did not live at home in term time: she lived in a student hall, where she shared a room meant for two with three other girls. This was better than living at home, as she was the eldest of ten, seven girls and three boys. Three were away at boarding school, but the remaining six lived with their parents, so there was little peace and no light to study at night as they did not have electricity.

'Aren't you lonely here all alone?' she wanted to know. 'Wouldn't you like someone to help you and keep you company?'

Others had already asked me this. They could not understand how anyone wanted to stay all alone in a house. It seemed strange even to me how much I enjoyed my solitary existence and the thought of anyone living here with me was intolerable. I did not even want a maid who would be in when I was not. The strength of this feeling surprised me, especially as it meant I had to do all my own housework, something I don't particularly enjoy. Seen through Rachel's eyes, it would have been ideal, if she could have stayed with me in the way younger children often went to live with their older siblings when they found jobs and housing elsewhere. I had a spare bedroom, there was space enough and light, when the power was on. I felt guilty, but I couldn't face sharing my house.

'I don't need any help, thank you, Rachel. I need to do the housework and gardening myself to get some exercise. Otherwise I'll just be sitting and reading or writing when I'm not teaching. I'm sorry. Also I'm expecting visitors and members of my family to come to stay some time, so it really isn't possible.'

The need for exercise was real enough, although walking to and from the classrooms and offices and sometimes the shop at the canteen provided some. The heat in the middle of the day was not conducive to physical activity and the cool hours in the mornings and evenings were all too brief.

Rachel asked if she could help me in any other way. I had an idea.

'Yes, I need to buy some things for the house and I'd like to see what they have in the market in Iganga. Would you be able to come with me and help with the shopping?'

She was delighted and we decided to go the next day.

When a very smartly dressed Rachel arrived in mid-morning, we had first to get *boda-bodas*. The carriers on these bicycles had removable padded PVC covers, offering a modicum of comfort for one's backside on the bumpy two mile ride to the tarmac road. There we could catch a minibus taxi for the half-hour drive to Iganga. Rachel was pleasant and useful company. She knew the correct fares for both kinds of taxi so we were not cheated. The motor taxis left town whenever they were full and, as we were not getting on at their starting point, one or two, already filled, left us standing. Eventually one stopped and allowed us to squeeze on the back seat. It was quite airy there as the back was open because the luggage space was too full to close it. These vehicles, generally poorly maintained, drove very fast, so it was good to be wedged in firmly, but conversation was impossible above the noise of the engine and the wind. The excellent road passed through a green patchwork of rice fields in the valleys with maize, cassava and a few banana plantations on the higher ground. Brown kites sat on the single telephone line, grey herons and white egrets rose from the fields as the taxi sped by. Goats and chickens had learned to keep off the road and the cattle were herded. We passed many houses along the road, some only half built, and several trading centres with shops, bicycle repairers, carpenters, small fruit and vegetable stalls and groups of *boda-bodas* waiting to carry people to more distant homesteads.

Iganga is on the busy Kenya to Kampala highway, which runs through the middle of the town. Three large roundabouts slowed down the lorries and tankers thundering past. Unattended cattle often grazed there, while goats wandered among the wrecked vehicles outside the police station. Away from the main road, the taxi park, the market, most of the *boda-bodas* and the bus park formed a bustling area where every space was occupied by some kind of business. Deafening music blared from loud-speakers outside the little shops drowning the traffic noise.

Our first port of call was the bank in the main street, where I had to open an account – a lengthy business. By the end we were hot and thirsty in spite of the fans whirring slowly in the banking hall. Rachel suggested a place where we could get a bottle of *soda*, the name for a variety of fizzy drinks, taken with a straw carefully shaken from its box, so as to be untouched by human hand. We sat at a table covered with a flowery plastic cloth and slightly protected from the clouds of dust outside by a net curtain. The ice cold drink was most welcome.

The covered market was enclosed by a wall. Rows of stalls were packed together, back to back, with the roofs above them almost meeting over the passageways for shoppers. They provided shade which was fine until it rained and shoppers became soaked from above and below where the water cascaded into the passages. There were sections for hardware, clothing, fish, meat and a variety of fruits and vegetables, nuts and pulses. An adjacent uncovered area accommodated sweet potatoes, cassava and large bunches of *matoke,* the green cooking bananas which were a very popular food. For some obscure reason pineapples were only sold in one corner outside the market. The sellers, men and women in roughly equal numbers, were friendly and curious, asking Rachel about me, if their English was not good enough to ask me directly. Rachel appeared to be unused to market shopping or prices, but she tried to haggle quite successfully. Bargaining was not very important, for which I was grateful, as I hated trying to beat people down from already low prices; on the other hand, I didn't like paying more than the going rate. Most items had a fairly regular price, higher only when supplies ran short.

Our shopping finished, we dragged the bulging baskets into a taxi for the return journey. Our problem began when we had to take our loads on the *boda-bodas*. It was not so easy to perch sideways on the carrier with a lumpy basket slipping off one's knees. In the end, we hired an extra bicycle to carry the shopping, for which the pad on the carrier was removed.

Rachel wanted me to meet her family. One afternoon she came to take me to her house. We went straight on where the wide track to the college swung round to the right behind my house and found ourselves on a narrow path through six foot high maize. The path skirted a few huts before coming out on the road which marked the edge of the college grounds. A hundred yards along on the opposite side, a huge house stood back from the road. Its appearance was deceptive because it had a second storey, unique in these rural parts. External stairs led to the upper floor where the family lived, in a room so crowded with beds that there was little room for chairs and only a small table. Mother, a smiling, round, comfortable woman, apologised for the lack of space.

'We have had to move the children in here as we keep the chickens in the bedrooms. When we had them outside, people stole them at night. This way is safer.'

The clucking, rustling and smell of the chickens pervaded the room. The children were all introduced, but disappeared outside again almost at once. Only two older girls stayed to talk to me, while Rachel and her mother made tea down below behind the house. The two youngest children kept peering in shyly from the top of the steps. The big girls told me about their activities. Then Father came home and talked about his work. As well as being a lecturer and having a parish, he was working on the first translation of the Bible into the local language, so he did not see much of his family. Grace was said before we had our cups of tea and small cakes. We chatted some more before it was time to go. After lengthy goodbyes two of the girls accompanied me almost back to my house, in accordance with their custom.

On her next visit Rachel brought a request.

'Mummy wants you to get her some oil and sugar.'

'How much does she want?'

'A can of oil and five kilos of sugar.'

'What sort of can? I buy oil in a bottle, so I don't know what you mean. How much?'

'A big one – ten litres.'

'That's a lot. What do you need so much for?'

'Mummy and I are going to make little cakes to sell to the student teachers to make some money for Christmas.'

It was clearly expected that I would provide these costly ingredients. I gave her the money to purchase the goods at the best price she could get, probably considerably less than it would have been for me. Christmas was an expensive feast for such a large family. Although no gifts were given, everyone had to have a new outfit for the celebrations and a good dinner.

As I had been away at Christmas, for the reasons given in the next chapter, the family invited me to spend New Year's Day with them. First I attended the church service, which was packed. Even more people went to church at New Year than at Christmas.

With great sincerity they thanked God for keeping them alive in the past year and prayed to survive the coming one. This awareness of the fragility of life was very striking. Survival was never taken for granted; even when people wished you a safe journey and return they really meant it – and with good reason.

At midday Rachel's sisters Agnes, Milly and Mebra, all in very fancy new dresses, came to collect me and we made our way through the maize which hid their home. They left me on a chair under a shady mango tree, always with one or more children to keep me company, while Rachel and her mother were busy preparing the meal behind the house. The three boys took their turn, too, at entertaining, but the two youngest girls who had performed brilliantly in my house a week earlier were shy and reluctant in front of their brothers and sisters. Later two women students came from the college with some exciting gossip about students who had been caught cheating in an exam. Unfortunately this was mainly discussed in the vernacular so I missed most of it. It was the middle of the afternoon before the students went and we were finally called to lunch up in the house, decorated with coloured streamers and pictures drawn by the children. Father was still absent on duty, but an aunt and a cousin were spending the holidays with the family, so the party numbered a good dozen. The dinner was the customary celebration meal: beef and chicken separate in tasty sauces, *matoke* (stewed banana), rice, potatoes, beans and cabbage. The potatoes, called Irish potatoes to distinguish them from the more common sweet ones, cooked with tomatoes and onions made a delicious dish. Plates were piled high as people have a large capacity because *matoke* and *posho*, the maize paste which is their normal diet, are not highly nutritious so quantity has to make up for quality. The younger children took their plates outside after the grace. Meals are usually taken in silence to concentrate on the food, but afterwards when the plates had been cleared, there was much chatter and laughter.

Eventually Daddy came home, with a photographer to record the occasion. He took pictures of everybody together, which was quite a feat, and then smaller groups and individuals. This was a lengthy business, and the sun was setting by the time the he had finished, so I had to go home. The girls came all the way with me again, after the rest of the family had said goodbye at the boundary of their land.

Over the next few months I saw Rachel quite often, but members of her family only rarely. Occasionally one of them needed a lift when I was going somewhere. Agnes passed her exams and went to a good boarding school to study for her 'A' Levels. Rachel was supposed to work hard for her final exams in June so I let her work in my house when I was out, but quite often I found her reading the newspaper when she should have been studying. Through her I learned a good deal about the life of the college as the students saw it, which was different from the impression given by staff. On one occasion I took her and another sister to Agnes's parents day at school. For various reasons there was not enough room for their mother to come too, so she asked me to talk to Agnes's teachers on her behalf. This may have been a good move as Agnes's report was not entirely favourable and she had a chance to do better before she had to face her parents – and she did improve.

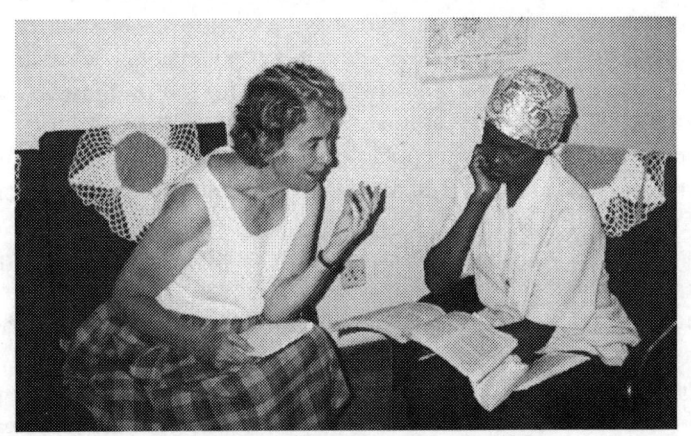

Agnes came for help with English

The school was situated on a high flat-topped hill with views to Lake Victoria. It was quite an old school, well built and well organised, as many of the older establishments were. Space for games and further development was limited by the site. It was an all girls boarding school with links with a similar boys school on a nearby hill. The only problem was the road up to it, which was extremely steep and weather-worn in the most precipitous places, but perhaps an advantage for a girls school in discouraging unwanted callers.

Agnes came to me for help during the holidays. English literature was her weakest and yet most important subject. I found it quite difficult to make useful suggestions, as the questions she had to answer were strange. A set type of answer seemed to be expected, but I did not know what. I probably did do her a service by getting her to read her set texts, as I learned later that this was not done as a matter of course. We also had some interesting discussions which can only have improved her English. She did eventually pass English with a good grade, which pleased us all.

Immediately after their exams in June, the secondary teachers left for seven weeks teaching practice in schools spread over most of the south-eastern part of the country. The primary teachers, in spite of the five years teaching experience they needed to get on the course, did supervised teaching practice at the same time, so staff were away on duty for four of those seven weeks, in a different area each week. It was a cumbersome system, but the best we could devise, given the need for careful supervision of staff as well as students. The preparation, in which I was heavily involved, kept me in the office long before we actually left the college. As a result I saw nothing of Rachel for several months. The students did not return to college after their teaching practice, but many stayed on in their practice schools as teachers until the end of the school year in December. Rachel managed to get a part-time job in one of the schools in the town. She rented a room there and took two of the younger children with her, so that they could attend a good fee-paying primary school. All this meant more expenditure for the family as Rachel's pay was barely enough to keep body and soul together. She had been very enterprising in matters financial, picking up an address from my table and writing a begging letter to my correspondent. I have to confess to being annoyed about this, but for her it was good, because when I confirmed that what she had written was true, she received £100 from my friend. Much of this she spent on fees for the two little ones and nothing on luxuries for herself. I visited her occasionally in town, but when she found a new job in January in a village some distance away I lost sight of her for long time.

9. MY CAR

After the chaos of the first few weeks while I settled into work and my house, a fairly regular routine developed with lectures on three days a week. It took time to get used to the two-hour sessions, but I often had the first at eight in the morning instead of a quarter to, because the students came late anyway. They were fresh then and it was cool – a good time to get work done, although I am not a morning person. On the other day in mid-week I did my washing, all of it by hand. I hung it out to dry on a wire stretched between the holey walls. In the middle of the day it dried very fast, at other times not at all. At a quarter to eleven the whole college had fifteen minutes break, when lecturers gathered in the staffroom and greeted each other by shaking hands all round before *dry tea*, (tea with sugar but no milk) and delicious roasted groundnuts were brought in. The newspaper arrived at this time and mail could be collected from the registrar's office. It was the time for news and gossip and I always made a point of being there. Staff also received a midday meal of *posho* and beans, but this often arrived very late and did not appeal to me anyway, so I had a snack at home. It was too hot to eat much in the middle of the day and I always cooked in the evening, afterwards doing all the washing up for the day to economise on water. Most afternoons I worked at home, marking, preparing lectures, reading or writing letters before gardening as the sun began to go down. Although I enjoyed this routine, I did feel a need to get away from it all at weekends, if only to talk colloquial English, which many at the college, even staff, found hard to follow.

Transport was a problem. I should have received a motorcycle for school visits and teaching practice supervision, though its use was restricted to one hundred mile journeys and forbidden in the capital unless you were an experienced motorcyclist. I did not qualify for a motorbike, as I had failed the necessary test in England. In fact, this was a relief as the motorcycle training in central Birmingham had been far more terrifying than anything I subsequently experienced in Africa. It was bad enough having to drive through the city centre in the morning rush hour in a car, but infinitely worse on two wheels not entirely under my control, following the instructor between huge lorries; or in four lanes of traffic on roundabouts, when the engine suddenly died; or being urged to go faster and faster on a dual carriageway when at forty miles an hour you already felt as if you were taking off into the blue. As I never really felt master of the machine, all the kindness, patience and enthusiasm of the instructors – and they were incredibly supportive – were finally wasted.

So here I was stuck in the bush with no transport of my own. Public transport was not bad. There were the *boda-bodas* for short journeys, such as into town or to the tarmac road. Riding on the back of a bicycle was surprisingly pleasant: cool and low-risk, being fairly slow and close to the ground, but carrying shopping could be a problem. For the longer journeys on the tarmac roads there were mini-buses, referred to as taxis. They were supposed to carry not more than fourteen passengers, but packed in more when off the main highway, where police checks were less common. They drove very fast despite their often dilapidated state and they operated without a timetable: they simply left when they were full. Road travel was probably the most dangerous feature of life in Uganda. One member of the college staff and several close relatives of lecturers lost their lives in accidents during my time there and many more deaths were reported. Various factors accounted for this: bad weather, poor road surfaces, lack of vehicle maintenance, bad driving, excessive speed and sometimes heavy traffic.

A car had always been at the back of my mind, but I wanted to see what the roads and the price of cars and petrol were like before I committed myself. As the main highway was in reasonable condition and the last twenty miles to the local town excellent, pothole-free, though straight and boring, I decided a small saloon car would be in order. When I mentioned my plan to purchase one at the college, everybody thanked me profusely. I wondered why, but soon found out. Another vehicle on campus was a public asset.

All cars available for sale were reconditioned imports. With the help of a local friend I chose a small four-door, four-seater Toyota Starlet imported from Japan to judge by the manual which no one could read. Insurance was prohibitively expensive, but so many horror stories of theft and accident were current that I thought it wisest to pay. I insured the car only for myself and members of my family to drive – a good move, as when I was asked to lend it, I had a ready excuse for refusing, which people accepted. I was also lucky in having a locked garage, where the car could not be seen, so no one thought about it. If I was going anywhere I told my neighbours and the office staff, who were often grateful for a lift. It was pleasant for me, too, to have company on longer journeys and useful for getting to know people better.

At first I expected that people would contribute to the petrol costs, which were high, but this only happened on the very rare occasions when I was specifically asked to do something on behalf of the college. Twice neighbours asked me to stand by at night, when people were very ill with malaria in case they needed to be taken to hospital, but this service was never actually required. On two occasions I was asked to act as ambulance in the day time, when there was no college transport available. Once when the pick-up which supplied the student canteen was off the road and the canteen had run out of beer and sodas my help was requested. That proved an interesting lesson in how things worked. I agreed to take as many crates of empty bottles as would fit into the car, but refused to bring back the same number of full ones because of the weight.

'That's not a problem,' said Mr. Musuki, who was also the canteen owner and pick-up driver. 'We can't get full bottles without returning the empties, but we can get the full crates back here without your help.'

We fitted in ten crates of empties. For the return journey, I only had four in the boot. The back of the car was filled with boxes of bread, toilet rolls, umbrellas and other small items. The remaining crates were sent back by taxi, loaded onto *boda-bodas* at the college turning and they were outside the canteen before we were, as the necessary negotiations and the other purchases had taken a good deal of time.

The greatest advantage of the car was the freedom it gave me to travel far and fast wherever I wanted to go. I felt the need to get away from the college at least every other weekend and many things could only be done in Kampala, where I stayed with my surrogate family. Being able to visit friends in their homes and otherwise inaccessible places in the bush with ease was an added attraction. One of these impromptu outings with a fellow volunteer one Sunday afternoon left a deep impression. We drove south from Iganga towards Lake Victoria just to see what was at the end of the road. It was quite a shock when we got there because the road ran straight into the lake on a sandy beach with a few houses up on the bank behind it. Some broken canoes lay in shallow water at the edge of the road, but no good ones were in sight. Swarms of ragged bare-foot children appeared and surrounded the car before we even had a chance to get out, but there was no sign of economic activity – no shops, no landing stage, at first, no adults. We walked to the edge of the water surrounded by up to sixty children, staring at us curiously. Eventually half a dozen men appeared from between the houses and one of them greeted us in English and asked us our business. We explained as best we could and asked him where all the children came from.

'They belong to us, the people of this village.'

'Is it a big village, then?'

'No. It's getting smaller. There is nothing to do here. People leave if they can find a job anywhere.'

'Are you not fishermen?'

'I teach in the primary school. My friends here no longer have any work. The fish have been poisoned. We cannot sell even the few we catch. Our land is farmed all the time and the crops are getting less and less. We have nothing to sell now. We get a little money when the contractors come with their lorries to get sand from over there behind the houses. That's all.'

'So how do you look after all these children? And what will happen when they grow up and produce yet more children?'

'It is difficult. We don't know what to do. Our gardens are already very small and now they are no longer producing well. What can we do? Can you help us to find work? Can you give us money for food?'

We explained that we were powerless to help and the only useful suggestion we could make was that they should try and limit the size of their families. They showed us round the sand pit and the poor mud houses, such as were often found on the lake shore serving as temporary shelters for fishermen, but here they were home to whole families. Barren and exposed to the full heat of the afternoon, the village did not even offer the shade of a tree. What does the future hold for such places?

Without the car it is unlikely that either of us would have seen this aspect of life in Uganda, as in our work we were always actively concerned with improving conditions. The ability to roam at will with my own transport certainly made an enormous difference to my knowledge, appreciation and enjoyment of the country.

The children who appeared at the edge of the lake

10. PRELUDE TO MALARIA

My arrival at the college coincided with the end of an unseasonable drought which left the campus brown and dusty. This soon changed to the opposite extreme when *El Nino* arrived with heavy storms and whole days of rain. Later I would have appreciated the attendant coolness, but at first only the sudden transformation of the land struck me. Everything turned green overnight. The people were not happy as they had not expected the rain and therefore had not planted their maize. They did it now in the rain, but there was so much that the crops were soon washed away – and not only the crops. The electricity supply became totally erratic as poles fell over in the swamps, which soon rose above the roads and washed them away. For a brief period not a single road for miles around was passable, even the main highway from Kenya was flooded in several places.

I had bought the car at the beginning of December and had every intention of spending my first Christmas at the college, but it was not to be. Coming back from Kampala a few days before the festival, I found the main road just outside Iganga a sea of stationary juggernauts and minibus taxis. The road had been washed away some days before and major repairs were in progress, with nothing allowed to pass. As soon as I stopped, three young men poked their heads through the passenger window.

'Where are you going? We can show you a way.'

I had been told that there was a route to the college via back roads, but I did not like the look of these characters, so I refused their offer. A minute later a schoolboy in a pink uniform shirt came along.

'I know the way. I will come with you.'

Just for the ride, I thought.

'How will you get back?' I asked him.

'It's not far. I'll walk... Are you from England?'

'Yes.'

'I would like to practise my English.'

He got in and we turned off the main road, passing close to where the railway line was suspended in mid-air, as the embankment had also disappeared in the floods. Finding the way was easy enough as the taxi drivers clearly knew about this route as well. Soon I found myself in a long queue of traffic on a narrow dirt road. The line ground to a halt. The lane was too narrow to cope with taxis and pick-ups in both directions, a bank on one side and a ditch on the other making it difficult to pass. Some men made an effort to get the vehicles from the opposite side through by moving us to one side as far as possible. When eventually nothing more came towards us, we still remained motionless. I left the boy, Moses, in the car and went to see what the problem was, causing quite a stir as a lone white woman here in the middle of nowhere. The road, such as it was, was slowly disintegrating into the papyrus swamp a little further on and had become completely impassable, in spite of the many hands willing to pull and push vehicles. Soon more men came round, this time to collect money to buy planks for a temporary bridge. The edge of the town and the tarmac road going north were only about half a mile ahead. After more than an hour nothing had changed.

Moses had run out of conversation long ago. We sat in silence until I shared a few bananas with him – the only food I had – before sending him on his way on foot, so that he would reach home before dark. I was now beginning to be concerned for myself. It would soon be dark. I hadn't had a proper meal all day, I was beginning to feel rather unwell and I didn't know what to do. In the end I decided to turn round and go back to Jinja, where I was certain of a roof over my head for the night. Everybody else of course had the same idea, and a tremendous scramble to turn round began. With my small car I was lucky and managed it quite quickly, but soon got caught up in the traffic at the back where the vehicles had more turning space. By the time I approached the main road it was pitch dark. Once again movement ahead was blocked. To make matters worse, I was feeling distinctly ill. Urgent knocking on the passenger window suddenly distracted me. A man wanted to know if I was going to Kampala. He needed a lift. I had been firmly told never to pick up strangers, as good Samaritans had sometimes been relieved of their cars – and worse. I knew it was risky, but I was desperate for company, in case I felt worse.

'I'm only going to Jinja.'

'That's fine. I can get another lift from there.'

My invisible passenger turned out to be a business man who had been trying to get through to the Kenyan border to lock a couple of open containers stuck on the railway, which had been washed away there as well. He spoke good English and talking with him took my mind off my discomfort.

Eventually we reached the main road, where chaos reigned: trucks and tankers were parked on both sides of the road, their drivers sitting under them, cooking their evening meal. In the narrow gap between them, taxis and cars were still driving aggressively towards Iganga. Travelling in the opposite direction, we had to cross the road before snaking our way through parked and moving vehicles and milling pedestrians. We were almost in the ditch and for a while off the road altogether until we cleared the parked lorries and buses. The thirty miles to Jinja passed without incident. My companion left me on the outskirts of the town, but not with the police patrol, who I thought could stop another lift for him. He preferred a deserted petrol station as, like most people, he feared the police. I was feeling so awful by this time, that it took me a whole hour to find the house I had visited only a few hours earlier.

I spent a pleasant Christmas there with English friends, still feeling ill on and off, before returning to my own house several days later.

In the middle of the morning after my return I collected my mail and made a drink. Suddenly I felt very hot, but my hands and feet were icy and I began to shake violently. This had to be malaria, in spite of all the pills I had been taking. I crawled next door and asked my neighbour to fetch the nurse. Both college nurses arrived in their smart white uniforms within twenty minutes. They confirmed malaria, injected me with chloroquine, washed me down with cold water and left me considerably more comfortable than they had found me. One of the nurses was Ruth, Paul's mother. She soon came back with tasty fresh passionfruit juice, which is supposed to bring the temperature down. Rachel appeared and suggested spending the night in my house with Ruth's eldest daughter Angela, an offer I was very happy to accept. Everybody was most kind and concerned. I went to bed at dusk and soon fell asleep to the sound of the girls' laughter and the drumming from the local station on my radio. They enjoyed a happy night with light and music, while I slept fairly soundly and woke up feeling much better.

Next day I dozed and read in an armchair rather than stay in bed, as it was cooler with both living room doors open and I could watch the comings and goings. In mid-afternoon two small girls appeared – Rachel's youngest sisters, Milly and Mebra, aged five and six. They looked very sweet in their Sunday-best lacy dresses with bows and frills. They were quite self-possessed although they only knew about a dozen words of English. Without saying anything, they began a fantastic entertainment. They sang together, they danced, then they took it in turns to sing and recite all the little English songs and rhymes they had learned in nursery school. Between acts they had brief whispered discussions and an occasional giggle, all the while watching me anxiously for approval. It was a delightful performance, and they kept it up for a whole hour before their parents arrived and eventually took them home.

By the evening I felt so much better that I declined company for the night. Next morning I was still a little shaky but otherwise completely recovered. Although I had several further attacks of malaria, I was never so ill again.

11. RUTH'S ENTERPRISE

When I arrived at the college, Ruth and her eight children lived just across the road. I saw some of the children occasionally, especially Paul, the second son, who became my water carrier. His two younger brothers sometimes came with him and occasionally they brought little Mary, the youngest. She was three, had a beautiful smile and went to the nursery, where I saw her quite often.

The family were still devastated by the death of their father which was veiled in a strange silence, but being new, I did not like to ask too many questions. Ruth herself was one of the two college nurses in the students' medical centre so we met sometimes on the road on our way to and from work. She was a tall, handsome, light-skinned woman, always smart, whether in her white uniform or a bright dress, and when she smiled she was beautiful.

When I had malaria Ruth kept a watchful eye on me, sending Angela, her eldest daughter, to look after me. She also came with me to the health centre to have the blood test when I was better. The road there was bad at the time, so we walked and had time for a long talk. Ruth was very concerned about her children still traumatised by their father's sudden death, especially Jane, the second daughter, whom he had taught at school. She was having inexplicable health problems, thought to be connected with her loss. This was serious because she was going into Senior 4 and would find it difficult to get good 'O' level results if she missed school. Angela, the eldest, had nearly finished her course at a primary teachers college, so she would soon be looking for a job. James was waiting for his 'O' Level results, not knowing what to do next, as now there was no money for him to go on studying. Another daughter had just finished Senior 1 and then there were the three boys in primary school and little Mary. They had also started building a big house in the village and Ruth had no idea how she was going to put all these children through school and finish the house without her husband's salary. She expected some insurance payment for him, but this could, and did in fact, take years to be paid. As if these problems were not enough, she was also likely to lose her job soon in another round of ancillary staff cuts, when the college ran short of money. These cuts seemed to happen fairly frequently and always affected the lowest paid workers, who had few, if any, other employment options. Academic staff were not made redundant.

When Ruth did lose her job and with it the staff house they all lived in, they stayed with relations not far away for a while. But Ruth urgently needed a home for her family and some sort of gainful employment and, being a trained nurse, she thought she could set up a small clinic in the next village. I offered to help her with the purchase of medicines, as there was little or no profit margin if she had to get them from Iganga in small quantities at short intervals. At first she asked for a very large sum of money to purchase them but when I pointed out that I was not a money tree and we costed her most urgent requirements, we worked out a viable scheme. We went to Iganga together to buy her first batch of medicines. Once I knew the shop and the staff there had met me, I could save her the journey and get the drugs when passing through. This never actually happened, as the German aid worker from the health centre offered to get the medicines from the wholesale distribution centre in Kampala which she used for her work.

Ruth rented a couple of rooms close to the road to the village. Angela meanwhile had found a teaching post away from home. She took the two youngest children to live with her near her school. Paul transferred along with a number of his class mates to a new private school in the town. Having spent more time at home being ill than she did at school, Jane had to repeat the class. Her younger sister like her boarded at school.

Although the older children had all learned English, they did not use it much and one had to speak very slowly and carefully so talking to them was not easy, but I was very fond of them. They never asked for anything, but did their work punctually, well and always with a smile. They never seemed to quarrel but helped each other when the need arose. For example, if Paul could not fetch the water, one of the others did it without involving me. I always felt that I could trust them. They were all such kind and pleasant people that I wanted to do whatever I could for them, such as putting James through the two-year motor mechanics course that he wanted to take at the technical college in Iganga. His exam results were quite good, so he had no difficulty in getting accepted.

One day I did ask Ruth what had happened to her husband on the night of his death after she had referred to it. I was deeply shocked when she claimed that he had been murdered by some of his colleagues, but she would not elaborate. I asked a number of people about the incident before I could piece together most of the story. Ruth's husband, by all accounts a well-loved and respected sober man and a good father, had visited a bar in town with friends one evening, as he often did. On the way back he joined the others in a bicycle race, an unusual thing for him to do. He was leading when he suddenly fell off. He was injured, apparently not too seriously and his friends helped him home, where his wife treated him. A little later he collapsed and was taken to the health centre, but he was too ill for the medical assistant's skill, so the director offered his pick-up to take him to the hospital in Iganga. He did not survive the journey. It was probably just a very unfortunate accident, or possibly there was some truth in Ruth's suspicion, that someone wished him harm and poisoned his drink. Such things were not unheard of.

With most of her family away, Ruth had time to try and get her clinic going, but success eluded her. Competition from other drug shops in the village and the town proved too great, and the people who lived nearby were the poorer ones. Ruth found it difficult not to help them when they were ill, but often they were unable to pay for their treatment. Where Ruth should have made a good profit, she made only a little. Then she was offered the job of nurse at the local technical school, potentially giving her a better income than she had received at the college. For a while all went well there, but soon her salary was no longer paid regularly and when she used her own drugs for the students, these were not paid for until months later. She kept her village clinic going for a while as often either James or Jane were at home to look after it when she had to be away. But when James went to Iganga and Jane eventually went back to school full time, Ruth was unable to keep the clinic. The rooms she rented were attached to a small private secondary school, which suddenly wanted them for staff accommodation, forcing her to move. Her new home was in the workers' housing of an abandoned coffee factory, just off the road, where it was quieter and safer, with friends and neighbours nearby, but they and some of our college students were her only clients. She kept the school job, but it was not a great help to her. She was always busy helping her neighbours with all sorts of jobs and I saw her less often.

12. SWAMP BAPTISM

On one occasion Ruth called round and eventually asked me if I would attend the baptism of her family the following Sunday afternoon. She wanted me to take pictures of the event, which I was very happy to do.

When she came on the day, she asked me to take the car. I was surprised, having expected the ceremony to take place somewhere in the college or in a chapel in town, so I wanted to know where we were going.

'To a certain place in the swamp near the railway line,' she answered.

'A swamp? Why? What are you going to do in the swamp?'

'We are Pentecostals and must be completely immersed in water in baptism,' she answered. 'Where else can we do that?'

We picked up the Reverend, Ruth's friend Nora and an old man at Ruth's brother's house and drove to the next village. There Ruth left us, saying she still had things to arrange and would meet us later. Where exactly were we to go? No one was quite sure, but a man offered to guide us. I refused to take more than three passengers, as we were to go down a track in the bush and I was concerned for my little car, especially as Nora was very matronly in her *busuti*. So the poor old man had to get out.

We set off down a narrow, badly rutted track at the back of the houses. I was very worried. The guide spoke little English, so the Reverend translated my concern. Fortunately this turned out to be a short cut leading to a reasonable road, which was said to be the right way. We drove for miles. At first plenty of houses stood in their gardens of banana and maize beside the well-used road. Then we came to a swamp, where the road had deep ruts, as is usual in such places. We inched our way through. At the next swamp crossing our guide hesitated, but remained fairly certain that we had not yet reached our destination, so on we went. There were now few houses and fewer people about. We reached a junction and another swamp stretched ahead of us, much wider this time, with the road disappearing over a rise on the far side.

Now it became quite obvious that our guide had no idea where we were. Fortunately a cyclist passed at that moment. He assured us that he knew where we were supposed to be: several miles back the way we had come. We had missed a left turn. We should have turned beside a very big house, which I remembered clearly. So we bumped our way back again.

When we reached the big house, we asked again and were directed down a narrow track.

'You can drive down there. It'll get wider, I expect,' the guide said.

I had my doubts. After about a hundred yards the track divided into three footpaths and even our guide conceded that the car could go no further. Nora and the Reverend got out and waited until I had parked back on the road before we set off on foot. The men wore proper shoes, my sandals were comfortable, but poor Nora had smart, wedge-heeled open shoes. These and her polyester *busuti* were far from ideal for a long afternoon walk under a cloudless sky.

It turned into a very long hike indeed, along a narrow path across some sandy patches where open shoes filled up with sand. It was hot, too, with only occasional trees for shade. Nora was beginning to struggle. At home in Jinja, a big town, where she worked as a school secretary, she was unaccustomed to trekking through the countryside. We had to walk in single file to avoid getting entangled in the wayside vegetation, having to get off the path altogether from time to time to make way for cyclists. While the Reverend and I got into a deep theological argument, which helped to keep our minds off the discomfort, Nora lagged further behind with the guide. After nearly an hour we reached the disused railway which crossed the district – and the edge of the swamp.

'At last we are nearly there,' we all thought happily. But no, we had to walk along the railway, which was even worse than the path, as the ballast on and beside the line was stony and rough and the sleepers were just too far apart for walking paces. We passed several spots of open water alongside the track, but these were not our destination. Eventually we saw a small crowd on the line. There a patch of brown water attractively framed by the delicate feathery green heads of papyrus showed on both sides of the line.

An enthusiastic welcome greeted the Reverend. Nora sank down on the line, her head in her hands.

'Are you all right?' I asked anxiously.

'Oh yes,' she said, 'but am I ever going to get back? I can't walk another step.'

'You'll feel better when you've had a rest,' I assured her, longing for a cold drink and a comfortable seat myself.

Things were beginning to happen now. A man clambered down the embankment to test the depth of the water and the group started to pray quietly. Suddenly we could hear singing and soon a procession came into view down the line. When they reached us the hymns gave way to excited greetings. Ruth's children came to greet Nora, who cheered up immediately, but made no attempt to get to her feet.

Soon the service began, with a short address by the Reverend followed by prayers and a long bible reading in the local language. More prayers and a hymn followed and then it was time for the actual baptism. The Reverend and another man stood up to their waists in the water in the middle of the clear patch. Another man nearer the edge helped the candidates to climb down and into the water. They came in order of age beginning with the oldest, an elderly man in a white *kanzu*, who seemed worried by the water. The Reverend said something to him and he replied and was instantly gripped by both shoulders, submerged backwards and brought straight up again, disorientated and spluttering. Firmly but gently he was passed back to the edge where willing hands helped him up the embankment.

The same procedure followed for another fifteen or so people, men and women, then girls and boys. Some struggled on their way down, some spluttered wildly as they came up out of the water, but there was complete silence and no laughter, however funny the ducking looked. Ruth and four of her eight children were among the candidates and I took pictures of them all as requested, hoping the photos had caught the right moment.

Michael being questioned before his baptism

All went smoothly until it got to Michael, the youngest and last. When the pastor spoke to him he did not answer. Again and again the Reverend asked him the question, but he just looked up at the crowd helplessly. Both men were now encouraging Michael to say whatever he had to and finally he, too, was immersed and came up with an enormous smile of relief. After a few more prayers and a rousing final hymn, it was all over. With much laughter the people milled about on the line, congratulating each other and exchanging news. Only Nora remained firmly seated while people came to talk to her.

Now it was time to go home. What was to be done about those of us who had to get back to the car? One of the organisers assured us that he could get bicycles to take us back, but along the railway we would have to walk. He shot off on his own bicycle alongside the track. Willing hands pulled Nora to her feet and slowly she limped back to the point where the path left the railway. There three men with bicycles were indeed waiting for us. We had to sit sideways on their carriers as usual, but these were not *boda-bodas* so the carriers were not padded and on the narrow and uneven path bouncing along on the bare metal was not particularly comfortable. In the sandy places we had to get off and walk, as even pushing the bicycles was not easy, but the return was much quicker and more pleasant than the outward journey. In the coolness of the late afternoon, we could appreciate our peaceful surroundings.

Back on the road, Nora sank gratefully into the car and revived remarkably. She was very happy that she had made this great effort to be with her friend on such an important occasion, although she had hardly had a chance to speak to her. She hoped we would all meet again soon. The others had already arrived back in the village. It was getting late and everyone wanted to get home before dark, so we all said fond farewells before going our separate ways.

13. BANANA TREE

Give me a spot
Where it's always hot.
In all of nature I must surely be
The most amazing, useful tree,
For the vast number of the gifts I give
To those who under my cool shadow live.
My leaves thatch roofs and can form walls,
Become umbrellas when rain falls,
Wrap meat for coolness and preserving,
And my own fruit for cooking and for serving.
My fibre tough is good as rope or string
And tied around my leaves makes many a thing,
Like baskets, balls, and pictures, mats for floors,
For sitting, sleeping on and use as doors.
In lavish hefty bunches grows my fruit
In many sizes, shapes and kinds to suit
Poor people's every need for food and drink:
Stewed it's *matoke*, a delicious food they think,
While raw it's sweet, yellow or sometimes pink;
Fermented it forms wondrous *waragi* and wine;
Even unwanted peel feeds cows and swine.
My stem can water for a drink produce;
Cut down, as props and seats it finds a use.
Bright with cut flowers planted on the way
To feasts and festivals, my suckers sway
And to the visitor are meant to say,
'Welcome! Enjoy yourself today.'
Now thank the Lord for making me
Such an amazing, useful tree.

14. ANNET'S DILEMMA

Outside the library a small, harassed woman with medium-length natural hair stopped me.

'Can I ask you something?' she murmured, her hands clasping and unclasping nervously.

'Of course,' I said.

'I've got a *supplementary*. I failed the paper you marked. Can you tell me where I went wrong?' Could I indeed? Without having taught the class, I had marked two hundred and forty scripts for these experienced primary teachers, who mostly found essay writing extremely difficult.

'What's your name?' I asked, not expecting that it would tell me anything.

'Nabirye Annet.'

'Come in here a moment and sit down, Annet,' I said, indicating the nearest empty classroom. This gave me a moment to think. It was quite likely that she had not really failed but been a victim of the highly irregular adjustment of my marks about which I had complained unsuccessfully to the powers that be. I could hardly tell her that..... so we settled for some general advice about reading the questions carefully and giving appropriate answers.

'Don't worry too much. I'm sure you'll be alright this time,' I finally said confidently.

'I don't know if I can do it at all,' Annet blurted out on the verge of tears, clasping and unclasping her hands again. Then the whole story poured out.

She was a primary teacher, recently widowed, with four children. She had to pay fees for the eldest, a girl, who was in Senior 2, with two years to go to 'O'Level, which would give her entry to primary teacher or nursing training, or a chance of acceptance for other vocational courses. Annet was having to pay for her own upgrading at the college and would have to pay extra for the re-sit. She was in the second year of her two-year Grade V Diploma course and had expected to finish that term, but the course had been extended by another term, which meant delay in getting her pay rise and further expenditure. She did not have enough money to pay her own and her daughter's fees for the current term. Either she would have to give up her course or she would have to take her daughter out of school. Leaving her course now would only increase her difficulties, as she would not qualify for the expected pay increase and she would have to repeat the whole year eventually, at even greater cost. Taking her daughter out would effectively end the girl's chances of a successful career, as she would almost certainly have to be married off in the next year or two. The next two children were in free primary school and the last in a nursery, for a small fee. Annet listed her income and expenditure. They were nowhere near balancing. What should she do?

'Well, I'll try and find someone in England to sponsor your daughter, but that will take time,' I promised. 'For now I'll give you your fees so that you can pay for your daughter. We'll see where we go from there.'

This time the tears came and I had to restrain her from going down on her knees in gratitude. Sponsors for her daughter and later for her son when he finished primary school were successfully found.

When Annet returned for the next term she was a different person. She had put on weight and smiles and moved with assurance. She often came to my house wanting to help me. We became good friends and I learned much about the college that I would never have discovered otherwise. As these students were salaried, some members of staff made money from them wherever they could. They offered them extra classes or booklets written by themselves which they claimed were essential for passing the exams. Through Annet I became involved in one such case. Arts and Crafts students were expected to produce a booklet about a craft of their choice. Typed, bound and non-returnable it had to be handed in as part of their examinable course work. As the cost of the typing and binding was enormous for people like Annet, she asked if I could type it for her. This exercise did not appear in any syllabus, so I had my suspicions, as the typing provided extra income for the secretary and the binding for the tutor in question. The students often had misgivings about such demands but were too worried about their results to protest and those who could not afford these extras failed to complete their diplomas. Soon after I started to type Annet's minimal script, the computer froze with the material in it. I informed her tutor, asking him to let me know when the work had to be handed in, so that we would not miss the deadline. It was never requested and I returned the draft to Annet after she had successfully completed the course.

As long as I was at the college we decided that I should keep the school fees money until it was needed. The first time I had given it to Annet at the end of term and was surprised to see her back a few weeks later. Could she have some more money? The original amount had been largely spent on fares when the whole family had to go to the distant funeral of a relative. In this way the immediate demands of the extended family frequently made a nonsense of planning. In fact, planning was simply not part of the scheme of things for anybody.

When Annet returned to her school after completing the course, I went to visit her, much to her delight. The school was near the top of a hill with superb views of Lake Victoria, deep blue beneath a lighter blue sky, and neat acres of brilliant green sugar plantation, between wedges of mixed farm and woodland, but getting there proved difficult. The track I was directed to was so steep and rutted that I abandoned the car on a playing field at the top and walked down. Eventually I spotted the bright dots of the children's uniforms on a big field next to shining corrugated iron roofs. Like almost every other primary school this one had half-finished classrooms and on-going construction work. In the afternoons the children's timetables included 'co-curricular activities', time often used for carrying bricks one at a time on their heads from the kiln to the building site. Some of the children were doing this when I arrived, while others were digging holes in the field.

Bringing the bricks for building the school

'Why are they doing that?' I asked.

'They will plant trees,' was the answer.

'That's excellent. You need to plant trees instead of just cutting for firewood all the time. It's good that you are teaching the children. They'll provide some good shade, too.'

'Our new head, Mr. Isabirye, is very keen on tree-planting,' said Annet, who had spotted me by this time. 'Would you like to meet him?'

We went to the Head's office. I still had some money for tree-planting raised by English school children when they were told about the loss of forest in Uganda. Mr. Isabirye was delighted when I offered to pay for some of the fruit trees they intended to plant to improve the children's diet.

Annet then asked me into her very basic home behind the headmaster's office: two tiny rooms with earth floors, a bed and a chair in each, a cot, a small rickety table and a few boxes with her household goods and clothes. The kitchen was an open grass-roofed shelter opposite the door. She shared this with another teacher. Annet lived here with her two younger children during term time. The youngest, a girl of about three, was in a dirty dress and covered in dust like everything else. She dissolved into tears when I spoke to her and needed her mother's encouragement and persuasion to take the sweets I offered her. The dust rose every time one moved, yet Annet was always spotless and neatly dressed, as were the children when they went to school. How they managed it in these surroundings where every drop of water had to carried some way up the hill is something I never understood.

Her diploma has enabled Annet to apply for promotion and when I was leaving she had applied for a deputy headship, which would mean a great improvement in her circumstances. Her daughter's fees are paid to the end of her course, while Peter, her son, has started at a secondary boarding school, where his fees so far have been met by English schoolgirls.

15. SCHOOLS

School practice, as it was called in the National Teachers Colleges, as opposed to *teaching practice* in primary teachers colleges, was probably the most interesting part of my job. Every tutor had to supervise a given number of students in each of the weeks allocated to teaching practice. The details of its organisation varied from year to year, but staff were keen to participate, because generous allowances were paid. In my first year both the primary and secondary teachers were on teaching practice for the same seven weeks in July and August, so some thirteen hundred students had to be allocated to suitable schools and then visited four times each. The schools were scattered all over the east and much of central Uganda, some in quite remote places, though road access to the school was a prerequisite for permission to use the school. Mr. Odongo, the School Practice Officer, an tall, imposing man who always called students *students*, was in charge of the office and David Mwanga and myself. We spent hours in the dim office at the end of a dark passage making endless lists recording which schools students would go to and who would supervise them each week. In my second year only the secondary teachers had to do teaching practice, making it much easier to organise. In that year the School Practice Office was allocated some money for a survey of the secondary schools used by students. They chose their own schools within given areas, preferably in groups of as many as the school could accommodate. We needed a clearer picture of which schools accepted our students and why and to encourage them to help the students to become good teachers, rather than gratefully use them as unpaid staff. For me it was a most interesting exercise.

The schools varied greatly in every respect from large well-established schools mostly in towns to tiny new ones starting up. A massive expansion in primary schools was under way as a result of the policy of universal free primary education which had been introduced two years earlier. Classes of a hundred or more children were the order of the day. In spite of this there were well organised schools and some excellent lessons. One I remember well because it got me into trouble for giving the student 90%, a mark considered far too high, as everybody was encouraged to give safe marks in the range of 45% to 70%, which would not attract the moderator's attention. This student read a story to a Primary 2 class of about seventy and then gave the children precise instructions how to act it in groups. They did this with enthusiasm and in a very orderly fashion, speaking clearly and listening to each other, much to the enjoyment of all. This school also had pictures and the children's work on the walls, which was not possible in other places where the termites had already eaten half the charts a student had made the previous week.

Some schools had even greater problems than termites, like a former army school where the garrison had moved on, leaving a block of three classrooms: one finished, one half built and the last one only foundations. The primary one class in the finished class room was very large and it was the only time I saw some very disturbed children. One began screaming and had to be removed while a head-banger was just accepted – 'He always does this,' they said. The upper classes were very much smaller, as many of the older children transferred to the big school in the nearby town as soon as they were old enough to walk the three miles there. Their lessons took place in a strange building: a central room with four very small ones leading off it. Classes of between twelve and twenty were so squashed in these little 'store' rooms that I could hardly find a seat. At least some groups could use the two proper classrooms in the afternoon, when the younger children had gone home.

A storm broke one afternoon while I was there. The rain blew in through the windows which had neither glass nor shutters. The rain came in through the roof, which threatened to come off altogether. Everybody crowded into the central area of the strange building but the wind blew the rain in through the open side. Staff and student teachers squeezed themselves against an outside wall on a bench under an overhanging roof out of the wind, the students frantically trying to keep their charts and books dry. Thus we waited until the rain almost stopped, before sliding through the mud to the road below.

'Do you always have such chaos when it rains?' I asked one of the regular teachers, as we watched drenched children slithering about.

'Oh, no,' came the answer, 'we normally send the pupils home when we see a storm coming.'

The town school that the older children went to was also extremely overcrowded. Over a hundred children in Primary 1 sat on the floor. It took the teacher ten minutes to give them all their exercise books and another ten to distribute their named pencils, another ten went on collecting everything up again at the end, which left ten minutes actual teaching time. How can anyone teach so many children to write sitting on the floor with barely space to put their books down? In Primary 2 it was marginally better. At least they had benches, though not quite enough. The teacher made the children kneel behind the benches, using them as desks, which seemed to make writing easier. On the whole the teachers worked hard, used their ingenuity and did their best in these difficult conditions. I was full of admiration for them.

A typical primary classroom

Primary schools did not have to be like this. Unconnected with my work at the college, I was invited to a private primary boarding school, recently founded by a Ugandan philanthropist. It was not easy to find the place hidden away behind a petrol station on a noisy pot-holed tarmac road in a busy township. Beyond the high wall and gate which separated it from the grim surroundings were solid but not opulent buildings neatly laid out round grassy areas. A child immediately asked me very politely what I wanted and took me to the headmaster's office. The purpose of the visit was to run a spelling competition for the top classes. While the pupils prepared, I looked at some of their exercise books. They were all neat, filled with uniformly clear, legible handwriting and all work had been marked and corrections done – most unusual. The children's spelling was even more amazing – better than that of the primary teachers in the college. The children themselves were calm and purposeful and the atmosphere was very business-like. The staff were enthusiastic and eager for any new ideas I could give them. The fees were not high but basic equipment was supplied and well used. Most unusually the school catered for the religious needs of all the major faiths: Catholic, Anglican and Muslim. Just before I left at dusk the Muslim children gathered for prayer. It was a little late and two small girls had already started before the rest. Kneeling on the path outside a classroom, they bowed down in the direction of Mecca while the other children just walked past them without any teasing.

Most secondary schools were private establishments run as businesses for profit for their owners, but even these varied greatly in their facilities and ethos. The government-sponsored schools, either in towns or established missionary foundations, were generally better. One of the worst secondary schools I saw was actually the very last one of all I visited. A small private school run by a young man whose own education had ended at 'O'level, it consisted of two or three shop rooms right up against a dusty road in the middle of a village with further rooms round a small courtyard behind. The latrines immediately beyond that were clearly inadequate for the number of pupils. The class I was to visit was in the courtyard, so we were spared the noise, dust and distraction of the road, but the room was so overfilled with children that the only space left for a chair was under the small blackboard, leaving the teacher access to only half of it. My offer to sit behind the door was turned down, as the door had to be kept open for ventilation. The first lesson was art: the pupils were to draw a hibiscus flower and the student teacher passed several samples round. The children were so tightly packed on benches, that they could hardly use their pencils let alone draw a plant in their scrappy exercise books, and the teacher could not look at their work, since no one could move. I did wonder what parents who paid hard-earned money for their children's schooling would say, if they saw these classes. In fact, they were probably happy that their offspring had found a place in a secondary school at all.

A few miles along the road in both directions were very different schools: one dating back to colonial times and the other quite new. Both had good buildings with large airy classrooms and at least some proper furniture and equipment. The old school, incidentally, was the only secondary school I came across, where the boys wore shorts instead of long trousers – a legacy from the past. Both of these schools also had proper timetables and bells when lessons ended, whereas in some schools it seemed to be guesswork that determined the length of a lesson. In other schools teachers were simply not in their classes, which, of course, became noisy and disturbed others. Classes of fifty secondary or a hundred primary pupils left to their own devices filled me with horror, but nothing seemed to happen. Eventually perhaps a senior member of staff might turn up and send the children out to play or home.

There are some excellent secondary schools with plenty of equipment and good facilities. The school where I had taught many years earlier, now considered the best in the country, was better endowed than many first world schools, with computers, science laboratories, a domestic science department with gas and electric cookers, a well-stocked library and a hall with tiered seating and a good stage. A school concert I attended there was better than anything our students were ever likely to see. The large sixth form had single or shared rooms such as our students only dreamed about. These schools also creamed off the best pupils in a kind of annual cattle market where heads bid for those with the best examination results. These heads were also extremely reluctant to accept our students for teaching practice. If they took students at all they preferred university ones. To some extent this was justified, as the English and general knowledge of many pupils exceeded that of our students, but it seemed a pity that the latter never experienced a really well run school. They themselves chose poor schools because they usually offered them free food and accommodation in return for using them as specialist subject teachers, often the only ones in the school. As a result the students received no guidance from experienced staff, but being retained and paid at the end of their course was obviously more important to them than learning to teach well – a dilemma which the college staff were unable to resolve.

Education generally seemed to be big business, with fees so high that the subsistence farmer parents often failed to find the money for more than one or two of their children to complete a course. The still widely held belief that going through school as far as possible was the key to a rich and happy future in a well paid job led parents to make enormous sacrifices. Law and Media Studies headed the list of favourite university courses, as neither required maths or science at 'A' level. Secondary and higher education yielded good incomes for their providers, but often not much chance for their students, as jobs in these favourite fields were few and hard to find. Teaching tended to be academic and theoretical, so practical courses were often inefficient and unpopular. The basic needs of the population were poorly served by the overfilled and academic primary syllabus and the seven years of schooling before assessment in the primary leaving examination. Four years of primary education starting at the age of seven or eight and focusing on basic skills: reading, writing, practical mathematics, health education, agriculture and useful crafts like carpentry, bicycle repair and home economics might have considerably more effect on poverty eradication.

Classrooms like this one with banana fibre walls should already be a thing of the past with the current primary school building programme

16. NOISES IN THE NIGHT

The college maintained a couple of night watchmen who patrolled the offices and student halls of residence, but the staff housing had no special security. My house had security lights at the front and back. Mr. Musuki, chief electrician in addition to all his other duties, had moved one of them from the garden door to between the bedroom windows. I never used it as the thin curtains did not keep the light out and I preferred to sleep in the dark. I asked Mr. Musuki a number of times over the next two years to put the light back in its original place so that I could see who knocked after dark, but he only did it shortly before I left. By that time it had occurred to me that the director had probably asked him to move it. It was all a little pointless as every other evening there was no electricity and quite often it was off all night as well. I slept soundly most of the time and never worried about robbers. The only time anything apart from garden produce was taken, it was soon returned. I came back one morning to find that I had left the big door slightly ajar and the pack of patience cards which I used all the time had gone from the coffee table. As nothing else was missing I suspected the nursery children, but before I had time to make enquiries, two of the occasional girl visitors came and returned the cards.

'We saw some boys at school playing with them. We thought they belonged to you, so we took them off the boys and here they are,' they told me.

'Which boys? How did they get them?'

But the girls would reveal no more and said they had to hurry back to school.

On another occasion I accidentally left the front door wide open with the key in the lock when I went away to a conference. I worried a good deal when I could not find my house key on the way home. As soon as I got back Mrs. Odongo presented me with it. After two days she had realised that I was not at home and had locked the door. Nothing was missing. I was delighted that I did not have to live behind high walls, protected by armed guards as many of my friends did.

Just occasionally fear struck. Drumming and shouting woke me one night during my first week at the college. It seemed to be coming from the classroom area. 'Good heavens, it's a riot,' I thought, and reached for my torch. It was just after six o'clock in the morning. The noise was rhythmic and seemed to be getting nearer. 'They're coming for me!' But that was not possible, I hadn't been there long enough to have had such an effect. The sound of drums and stamping feet accompanied by a sort of chant was definitely approaching from the direction of the college. Then suddenly it veered and took another direction until it faded into the distance. Later I discovered that some students had decided to go jogging at six o'clock one morning a week to increase their fitness, and drums and songs usually accompanied such activities. They soon lost interest in this commendable exercise, and no more drums sounded at dawn.

Just before Christmas I thought I was dreaming of home when I woke to the sound of carol singing at dawn. The faint singing came from one of the classrooms where students had gathered for an early morning service. Their discos in the dining hall were noisier affairs with a beat which shook the ground even in my house a quarter of a mile away. Although I was often invited to these functions, the volume of sound always put me off before I got there. It was loud enough in my house. Other neighbours, especially those with small children, also found it a little too much, and eventually it was agreed that the amplifiers should be turned down at midnight.

By the time we really had a riot I was no longer afraid. I came home at dusk after a late lecture with Okello, one of the students, who was collecting the video player and a Shakespeare film for the English students. By the time he left, it was nearly dark and another knock on the door surprised me.

'Lock your door and keep it locked,' said Mrs Odongo urgently. 'The students are rioting.'

With that she disappeared into the night. It seemed incredible. Half an hour earlier only a handful of students had stood by the big notice board which carried all information relevant to them. The rest of the college seemed deserted as usual at this hour. What could have happened? Now drumming could be heard in the distance and then shouting. I locked my door and started my evening meal. As there was no electricity that night, everywhere was in darkness except for feeble lamplight in the houses. Suddenly I heard voices outside followed by urgent knocking on my door.

'Open, Madam. Let us in. We've got the video.'

I opened the door and there stood Okello accompanied by three friends whom I did not know.

'May we come in? Can you hide us? We've brought back the video. We thought it wouldn't be safe in the Guild House. Can anyone see us in here? Where can we go?'

'Come in. Who are you hiding from? What on earth is going on?' I took the video from them. 'Sit down and tell me what all this is about.'

'Some of the students are rioting. We didn't want to join in, but they'll beat us if they find us here.'

By this time the noise was getting louder and nearer.

'They're coming this way. They're going to the director's house. Where can we go?'

'Don't worry,' I said. 'Look, if they come to the front door you can escape through my bedroom window. They won't see you. If they come from the back, you can go in the garage. Now, for goodness sake, tell me what's happening.'

The lads calmed down after I had shown them their escape route and Okello explained.

'A notice from the Ministry of Education went up on the board this evening, saying we must all pay more money towards our teaching practice. How can we find money between now and next term, when our parents have to pay school fees for the other children as well? They should at least have warned us earlier.

The students are angry and are blaming the director for all our money that goes missing. We shouldn't have to pay any more.'

By this time it was clear that the rioters were coming down the road at the front in large numbers. They were noisy but sounded quite orderly – no attacks on lecturers' houses, no cracking of branches from the hedges. Everybody seemed to be on the road. I moved the lamp to the table by the window.

'Just sit still. No one can see you in here. If anybody does come to the door, you know where to go,' I said to the lads, not feeling particularly worried for myself.

The crowd approached with threatening drumbeat and angry shouting. The tension rose when tremendous crashes came from the director's compound. The rioters were stoning the big corrugated iron door of the garage where the college lorry was kept. It made a satisfyingly vicious din for about five minutes. Then the students withdrew round the back of my house towards the college. The noise receded and before long silence reigned once again on the campus. After a further few minutes I opened the front door. Not a soul was in sight so my visitors could leave with little risk of detection, let alone attack, on the way to their hall of residence.

What did annoy me was the certainty that the next day's lectures would be cancelled and time to make them up had run out. Sure enough the drama continued next morning. The students demanded to speak to the director, who, like the staff, had been tipped off the night before. He had gone to town to alert the police, although he was anxious to keep them out of the college if possible, as they were likely to shoot when confronted with a noisy crowd. He agreed to talk to the students. A period of quiet expectancy followed, as a group of rioters had gone to town to enlist sympathy in the local schools and their return had to be awaited. When they came back an interminable session with the director and senior staff and most of the students took place in neutral territory under a big mango tree. The riot leaders, it seemed, had made some basic errors in planning when they proposed a hunger strike. After they themselves had eaten the night before they had kept the rest of the students from their evening meal by force. They also banned breakfast, so by midday hunger and heat overcame most students and they just drifted away when no room was left in the shrinking shade. The lack of animosity and positive friendliness towards members of staff surprised me. The grievances were almost exclusively financial and thus only concerned the administration.

Rioting students meet senior staff under the mango tree

On another occasion my colleague from next door called in at dusk. He was clearly upset and readily accepted a cup of tea before telling me that one of his children, a seven-year-old girl, was not expected to live through the night. She had been hospitalised at the health centre for nearly two weeks. At first it was thought she had malaria, but when she did not respond to treatment, they found too late that she had meningitis. He had come to tell me this because people were likely to be moving around during the night coming to his house. He did not want me to be frightened, which was very thoughtful of him. Sure enough I was woken at some point by torchlight shining in through the bedroom window as men walked through my garden. I heard people go in next door, then talking and furniture being moved. Although I heard no one else arrive, suddenly someone began to wail loudly and other people joined in. The keening continued with brief intervals for about an hour, after which silence returned. The poor little girl had died.

On another occasion I did get worried. I always went to bed late unlike most of the people round me. One night just after I had gone to bed around midnight a lot of shouting and screaming, including children's voices, suddenly started. It seemed to come from the villagers' houses on the boundary road. Drums and gongs joined in and what sounded like a very large crowd milled around making a tremendous din before drifting away into the distance. No one stirred in the college houses, which was reassuring. Next morning when I asked what had happened, it took time to find someone who had heard anything. One neighbour thought that a shooting star had appeared to come down at the edge of the village, so everyone had to get up and make as much noise as possible to chase away the evil spirits which came from the sky.

Not all the night noises were made by humans. In the rainy season frogs and toads croaked lustily and at all times insects chirped and small creatures rustled about outside. I was less happy when I heard tiny feet patter over the mosquito mesh on the windows. They were probably lizards rather than rats but it was impossible to tell whether they were outside or in. I did once find one of the common dark grey lizards with a white stripe curled up in my bed between the sheet and blanket, after which I always checked the bed before getting in. Sometimes dogs howled in the village. On moonlit nights birds mating in the eucalyptus trees beyond my garden flapped about noisily, and occasionally I heard owls. Once one sitting on the garden wall had a long delightful conversation with another a little further away.

Generally, in spite of the large number of people living in close proximity, the nights were extraordinarily still. Human sounds were rare – a baby crying, perhaps, for a moment. Sound carried a long way so a lorry or car could be heard from miles away, but there was little enough traffic in the day and virtually none at night. The silence and the moonlight were very special.

17. MURCHISON FALLS

Every visitor to Uganda wants to go to a game park. My son Christopher was no exception, but much of Uganda was out of bounds to us on security grounds and even more at the time he came because many roads had been washed away by the storms of *El Nino*.

Moreover, as his visit coincided with term time, I had to free a very long weekend before we could set off for Murchison Falls National Park, renowned for the spectacular falls on the Nile which give it its name, and once the home of large herds of elephants and other big game. We did not know if we would find any animals; in fact, it was not certain that we would even reach the park. As it was impossible to get in touch with anyone, we had to hope that one of two volunteer friends in Masindi would be able to put us up for the night and give us reliable information about the state of the road into the park. The main road to Masindi was still under water, but we hoped to use an alternative route on a minor road.

We set off in high hopes. It had not rained for two days at our starting point, so there was a chance that roads elsewhere were drying out too. The first hundred and fifty miles from Kampala were good tarmac road. The normal *murram* route to Masindi being still impassable, we found the other road and decided to try it. It took us through rolling cultivated countryside with dark clouds once more lowering overhead. The slippery wet surface meant slow progress and we had to beware of patches of deep mud and the ruts left by heavy vehicles, but we managed to reach Masindi just as the rain started to fall again. We drove through the rather uninspiring town to the Teachers College on the outskirts. I had stayed with Sally, a fellow volunteer, before and had no trouble finding her house on the tree-studded campus. The door, which led directly into the sitting room, was opened by Johnny, her houseboy, to reveal about twenty children sitting on the floor watching television. Sally was away and Johnny did not appear to relish the prospect of us staying in her house.

'Stay in Kate's house. Teresa next door has the key,' he told us. Kate was a volunteer from my group, so I was sure she would not mind.

'When will Sally be back?'

'Next week.'

'And Kate?'

'Monday, or even later.'

Bad luck for us. Fortunately Teresa next door, a teacher, was in and happy to let us into Kate's house. She assured us that she had been to the Game Park and that we would be alright on the main track, if the park authorities allowed us in. She told us how to find the entrance, which was further from the town than I thought.

We set off early next morning in fine weather and reached the park entrance without difficulty. After paying our fees we agreed to take a young woman park worker with us. She needed to go to Paraa on the other side of the Nile, while we were hoping to reach the park office by the river to arrange a boat trip for the next day. The road was now a single track through the bush, with no views as the low trees and shrubs came right to the edge of the road, and there were no animals. Little cars like mine did not often come here. For much of the way the track consisted of two deep ruts made by lorries and landrovers. The raised centre constituted a constant danger to our sump, made worse by the extra inches added by incipient termite mounds at intervals along this ridge. Great care was required to keep out of the ruts, with one wheel on the edge of the road and the other in the centre. The heat in the black car became unbearable, as we had to keep the windows shut to keep out swarms of tsetse flies and the air conditioning did not function at such a low speed. Then we came to the first really bad patch, where a big vehicle had got stuck and chewed up the track. We had to stop and fill the ruts with lumps of mud and dead branches. Our passenger thought this most amusing: two *wazungu* labouring on the road. She had to get out too and walk over the worst bits while one of us drove. One spot looked so difficult that we nearly gave up, but by then it would have been as bad to turn back as to go on.

Eventually the scrub gave way to grassland and the track improved. The grass, long and green after the rain, shimmered under the sun in the brilliantly clear air, with the wind ruffling it in shining waves while the roadside glittered with the flowers of golden *bidens*, orange *leonotis*, purple *vernonia* and the occasional patch of small scarlet-flowered hibiscus. Strange sausage trees, with fruits dangling like giant sausages from the bare branches, giving them their name, and other big trees dotted the landscape. Doves and small bright birds darted across the road and we drove through a troupe of baboons, but saw no big game.

Progress was still quite slow and it was mid-afternoon before we reached the park office near the Nile where we left our passenger and booked places on the launch for the round trip to the Murchison Falls the next morning. We had also used considerably more petrol than I had anticipated and needed a top-up to be sure of getting back to Masindi. We negotiated with the park staff and they agreed to send someone to the other side where he could get a jerry can full. This was very expensive and, with my paranoia about carrying cash, left us almost penniless. I just hoped that one of my friends would be back in Masindi and able to lend us some money on our return.

Then we went in search of the nearby camp site. *Bandas*, little round huts, were available, but Chris had borrowed a light-weight dome tent, so we decided to use it. There were toilets and showers and a bigger building housing the office, stores and kitchen, with a large covered dining area attached. Here we enjoyed a cold beer before pitching the tent, leaving off the fly sheet for maximum air circulation. We also brushed the worst of the dust off the car, showered and changed for the dinner we had ordered before going back to the park office to collect our petrol. Other people were arriving in land cruisers and lorries and our little car received some funny looks. Quite a crowd gathered for dinner and the serving took time, but at the end we were pleasantly surprised to be moved to one side for an entertainment.

Colourful dancers and musicians of the Acholi and Langi tribes displayed their dances. They were mostly members of the park staff and their families who were being specially trained to perform in order to give them some additional income when they had perfected their programme. This practice performance of the vigorous dances was already most enjoyable, especially in the relaxed atmosphere with locals as well as visitors making up the audience, all contributing willingly when a hat was passed round at the end. Going to bed we could hear a few hippo grunting in the distance, but otherwise nothing more exciting than the usual nightly chirping of thousands of insects.

Straight after breakfast next morning we went down to the river to board the launch which was to take us upstream to the bottom of the falls. The river was so wide that it was difficult to make out the elephants grazing on the opposite bank. We were only a handful of passengers with plenty of room on the two decks – the top one open to the sun, the lower providing some shade. The river looked very placid but once we started we could feel the powerful current as we struggled upstream against it. The launch made for the opposite bank, where the ground rose away from the river and we soon saw families of hippos of all sizes basking in the shallow water near the edge or grazing on the bank and dashing into the water as the boat approached. Crocodiles lying well camouflaged and motionless on the sand at the water's edge were difficult to spot. We saw a few more elephants in the distance and many birds from big saddle-billed storks and herons to tiny bright scarlet sunbirds. Progress was leisurely and the boat slowed when there was anything to see on the bank. Islands of vegetation drifted down the river along with shredded water hyacinth, the weed which caused havoc in Lakes Victoria and Kyoga with its rampant growth, but which had been chewed up by the falls and mercifully could not survive in running water.

After about an hour we seemed to be entering a lake with a high bank at the end. It was not until we were much closer to the bank that we could make out the falls, a tiny white streak in the distance. This grew as we approached a rocky island in midstream. The guide explained that we could go no further as the river narrowed here and the current was too strong. The launch pulled in very close to the rock and from the stern we had a good view of the vast volume of yellowish water thundering through a rocky gap behind a curtain of spray which held a brilliant rainbow. We stayed for a while admiring the awesome scene, the water swirling white around us below the high bank covered in dense dark green vegetation. Then it was time to turn round. Downstream we moved rather faster and away from the bank, but at one stage we pulled into one of the mid-stream islands of papyrus and reeds. The guide went over the side of the boat working his way round to the back where he had to dive in order to free the propeller which had become clogged with vegetation.

The top of Murchison Falls

By mid-morning we were back at the landing stage. We had to get back to Kampala that night and were concerned about the very bad spot on the road back. However, we thought we had time to drive to the top of the falls. Once we branched off the road on which we had come in, the track deteriorated and eventually became so boulder-strewn that we decided to walk the rest of the way. We could already hear the falls thundering ahead and below us. It took us about half an hour to get to the camp site and buildings at the top of the falls from where we could see nothing. A game ranger offered to guide us around the top of the falls. A well maintained and protected path led some way down to a place from which both arms of the falls were visible with the water tumbling over the edge in its turbulent descent. The noise was deafening; the force of the water awe-inspiring, as the recent floods provided a particularly impressive volume of water.

At about three o'clock we were back at the camp site. A large four-wheel-drive vehicle with diplomatic number plates was just leaving with a family of four. We would have been delighted if they had offered us a lift instead of leaving us worried whether they would be able to pass our car, parked beside the narrow track. Instead we were approached by a young park ranger.

'Could you possibly give me a lift?'

'Where do you want to go?'

'To Masindi. I've got some leave and I've already waited three days to get away from here.'

'You are welcome to come with us,' I said, quite pleased at the thought of a strong man to help if we had trouble with the road again, 'but we have left our car some way up the road. We'll have to walk back to it.'

'That's OK, thank you please. Let me just get my things.'

So we walked up the hill together in the hot afternoon sun and managed to drive back without difficulty even with the added weight of our passenger. Just as we were approaching the junction with the main track a wart hog crossed in front of us and disappeared into the long grass. The ranger encouraged us to get out to have a closer look at the creature. At the point where it had disappeared, we saw it enter a bare patch of ground where two buffalo were sunning themselves. We did not stay to see any more. Buffalo are among the most aggressive and dangerous animals in the wild, and we wanted no trouble, especially as the track curved round this spot so we had to pass close to them in the car.

The next problem was the bad spot. To our amazement it had disappeared. The road had been repaired there and in one or two other places as well during the day and a half since we had come in, so the return journey was faster and less harrowing. We stopped briefly at a game rangers' camp where our passenger wanted to greet his friends. He left us at the park gate.

Back in Masindi at about five we found that neither of my friends had returned. We urgently needed fuel to get back to Kampala but had insufficient cash. We went to the petrol station to see what kind of deal we could do. I parked by a pump but asked the attendant not to fill up the car until I had seen the manager. Chris had some English money, but as it was Sunday afternoon there was no hope of changing it. When we explained our predicament to the manager he was most helpful and immediately agreed to allow us to pay in English pounds at the normal exchange rate. We were most grateful for his kindness. It was also just as well, as the pump attendant had filled up the car until it could not take another drop and we barely had enough to pay for it with the money we had changed. We returned safely to Kampala, where I was at last able to borrow some money until I could get to my bank in Iganga.

18. ALICE'S DUPLICITY

Late one afternoon a tall attractive girl in a low-cut blouse appeared at the back door. I did not know Alice although she lived only a few doors away with her sister Susan and brother-in-law George. She came in, sat down confidently in an armchair and told me about herself. She was in the 'O' Level class at the nearest good secondary school. George, one of my colleagues, had been paying her fees, but found this difficult as he had four children of his own and was also supporting other relations. She did not labour the point and I chose to ignore it. She then launched into a vivid account of Karamojong cattle raiders attacking her home village in Katakwi District in the north east.

'If they come in the day sometimes you can run away and hide in the long grass. If they come at night it's really bad. They take all your cattle and goats first. Then they burst in with their guns. They make you pack up all your things and carry them, as they drive you like the cattle to their trucks. If you don't do what they want or walk too slowly, they shoot you. They make you pile all the things in the truck with the cows and goats and even the chickens and then they drive off.'

'Did this actually happen to you?'

'We always managed to escape, but it happened to our neighbours.'

Then she asked if I would help her with her English for the exams as she was often unable to go to school, because she had to stay at home to mind her sister's baby. I had already heard that Susan had recently disappeared under rather mysterious circumstances when she and Alice were on the way to visit their parents. She had got off the bus in one of the towns and not returned to it. Alice travelled on to the next town with the baby and then contacted George because she did not know what to do when Susan failed to arrive on the next bus. He told her to come home. Later George visited their village and his own, but found no trace of Susan. He searched intermittently for about six weeks. It was not a happy situation, as the year-old baby was ill much of the time, no doubt missing his mother. Alice was a reluctant substitute and upset about having to sleep with the child. It occurred to me that she had come round mainly to escape from home.

Susan eventually returned. No one would tell me a coherent story about what had happened, but Alice came more often now, complaining bitterly about the atmosphere at home. Everybody was horrid to her. She had no idea why. They said nasty things about her behind her back and often to her face. She openly stated that she saw my house as a kind of refuge from her own, but she was always anxious that no one should see her coming. I kept my ears open to the endless gossip, but heard nothing that threw any light on the situation.

One evening about this time a young man came round. It turned out that Daudi was George's nephew, who lived in the same house. He had heard that I was going to his home area to supervise teaching practice. Could I take a letter to his father? He was desperate to go home. He was also in his 'O'level year in a different school from Alice and one where he was unlikely to achieve good results. Life in his uncle's house was so unpleasant that he just wanted to go home. He would not elaborate on what was wrong, and swore me to secrecy, as he did not want his uncle to know that he was complaining. He gave me his father's address and instructions in writing how to find his house. These were still on the table, when George himself arrived to discuss our travel arrangements, as he was coming with me. He must have noticed the paper, but he said nothing. In fact, nothing at all happened, as I did not have time to find Daudi's father while we were away and the matter was never mentioned again.

Shortly after this Alice turned up with her arm in a sling.

'Whatever has happened to you?' I asked, hoping that this was not the result of domestic violence.

'A woman on a scooter knocked me off my bicycle when I was coming back from school today.'

'Where did that happen?'

'On the road from town. She was going the other way. She lost control and crashed into me sideways.'

'Was she alright?'

'Yes, I think so. She was the head teacher of Kititi school. It was all her fault.'

'Will anybody believe that?'

'Oh yes. Plenty of people saw what happened and they helped me. The bicycle is broken. They helped me back. My shoulder hurts and here I have a cut on my arm.'

The wound did not look serious. Her sister was a nurse, so there was no need for me to do anything about her injuries except to commiserate and suggest she go home and get some sleep.

The next evening she was back, in tears.

'My arm hurts so much, and my sister won't even give me an aspirin. She hates me and blames me for everything. She thinks I am trying to take her husband away from her. He runs after me. I don't know what to do. They all hate me.'

I made her a cup of tea and gave her some aspirin, while she told me that she had been to the doctor and to the police about the accident. No serious damage had been done. The next evening she came again, even more upset. Her sister had taken some of her clothes away and she had pushed her on her bad arm.

'I think she is trying to kill me.'

This was worrying. Although the holidays were about to start, Alice, being in the exam class, would be expected to keep going to school. She had to get away from home, where relationships were clearly out of hand, but where could she go? Then I thought of Rachel, who had a room in town. Perhaps she could put her up for a couple of weeks. I told Alice I would see what I could do, but she was not to tell anybody about our plan.

On the way back from seeing Rachel, who readily agreed to help, I gave a lift to one of my few female colleagues. I asked her if she knew what was going on with my neighbours, but all she would say was, 'That Alice, she is a bad girl. Don't help her, she's a bad girl.'

No amount of questioning could get any more out of her, but by this time I was beginning to put two and two together and could guess what Susan was saying about her sister. But what was the truth?

When I told Alice that I had found a place for her, we arranged that I would take her next morning. She would bring some things to leave in my house and be ready with her bag, when I drove by.

Next morning I found a cardboard box with old school books and a bag I had given Alice outside the back door. I had just put them in the store when Susan appeared at the front door. Unlike pretty Alice, Susan was never smart. Now, as usual, she was in her working clothes, though unusually with no children in tow, and she was clearly deeply upset.

'You are taking my sister away, aren't you?' she asked after a perfunctory greeting.

'Yes.'

'Where are you taking her?'

'I don't want to tell you. I think it's better if she is out of the way and nobody knows where she is. Then you can sort out your problems in peace.'

Then she poured out her side of the story. She had brought her little sister from home years ago, so that she could get a good education. She had clothed her and fed her, and what thanks did she get? Her sister was now trying to take her husband away from her, the father of her children. Her husband had neither eyes nor time for anyone but Alice and if she complained about Susan her husband beat her, so she had a right to know where Alice was going.

'No one will know where Alice is. She is not going home and she is not going very far from here. More I am not prepared to say. I think it's better if you don't know.'

That seemed to calm her a little. Perhaps she had been afraid that Alice would go home and tell their parents all sorts of lies about her.

'Alice is taking some of my things away, isn't she?' was her next line of attack.

'I don't think so,' I answered. 'You can see what she is leaving here.'

I fetched the box and the bag, knowing that this was not what she had expected.

'That's alright,' she said, defeated. 'O.K. Take her away as well. I'm sorry I bothered you.'

I felt dreadfully sorry for her. She was obviously not the monster Alice had made her out to be, and it was equally clear that they had grown to hate each other fiercely. It seemed extraordinary to get drawn into an intimate family affair in such a different culture. I became rather concerned about my own position in this drama, as violence in such situations was not uncommon.

Susan left and a little later I took Alice to town.

It was lucky that next morning I was giving a lift to Odongo, our neighbour and a colleague whom I knew quite well. Here was a chance to find out a bit more, perhaps. I was sure that he didn't need me to tell him what had been going on because it was probably common knowledge.

'George is actually one of my cousins; our fathers are brothers,' he told me. 'So we know that he is after Alice and ill-treats his wife. In fact Susan slept in our house last night because George came back from the canteen late and tried to beat her. There is a lot of trouble in that house. My wife and I have both spoken to him several times. What he's doing is not good. But he will not listen.'

'I feel bad about interfering in their family affairs. What do you think?' And I told him what I had done.

'If you can keep Alice away that's very good. Don't worry. Do what you can.'

So Alice was temporarily removed from the scene. It had already been agreed that she would board at school for her last term with George paying her fees. After that she would go home to her village. I checked on her once at Rachel's before I went on leave, hoping that would be the end of my involvement in my neighbours' affairs.

On my return a month later I went to see Rachel. Everything had gone according to plan and there had been no problems. I heard nothing from Alice until she sent a letter almost at the end of the term. Could she possibly have a little pocket money for paper and a bit of extra food? I sent her that, in spite of hearing rumours that she was still seeing George. Another letter arrived the day before the end of term. Could I pick her up from school the next day? I had already arranged something else that day and would not be back in time. I sent my apologies with the boy who had brought her note. I expected to see Alice that evening, but she did not appear for several days. In the meantime I heard that she had fallen off a *boda-boda* in town. When she came she told me she had gone to a brother in Iganga after leaving school. Now she wanted to discuss her future. I promised to try and find her a place for training of some sort and to help with the cost, provided she kept well away from the college and her brother-in-law. She was to stay at home and make herself useful until her results came out. If she could find a suitable opening in Soroti, the nearest town to her home, she should let me know. I sent her off with her bus fare and some extra money to see if she could do a little trading in her home area.

Six weeks later, well before the exam results were due, there was a knock on the door after dark one night and Alice slipped in.

'I don't want anybody to know that I'm here, especially not them.' She pointed in the direction of her house. 'I'll go again first thing in the morning and nobody need know I have been here.'

'But why *are* you here?' I wanted to know. 'I haven't written to you. You haven't had any results yet. Why have you come?'

'I thought you had found a place for me.'

'You know that isn't possible till you have your results. I am not happy that you have come all this way. Who paid for you?'

'I borrowed the money from my father, but I must pay it back.'

Fine, I thought, just shake the money tree and you'll be alright!

'And do you really think that no one saw you come and that you can leave without being seen? In this place?'

'Well, I don't know. I did try.'

She stayed in the spare bedroom all the following day, because it was already light when she got up, but she did leave early on the morning after, with her expensive return fare and firm instructions not to appear again until she heard from me.

Finding any kind of training place that I could afford was a problem. There were plenty of private institutions for business studies, her preferred option, and hotel and tourist work, but they were all very costly. Soon a letter came from Alice. She had got a place in a secretarial school in Soroti. She sent some details, but when I made enquiries it turned out that the school probably only existed on paper and once she, or rather I, had paid her fees there would be no classes. When I told George about this he made no comment, but a little later another member of staff asked me if I knew of a place where Alice could go for training in Jinja; George had asked him to find something for her. I told him what I knew and he promised to do no more. At this time I was also looking at places for Joe – more about him follows – and ended up by taking him to a computer college in Iganga. This two-roomed establishment just off the main street had two computers and four desks, an impressive syllabus and high fees for a two year course – a long period of study before any qualification was offered. As it was well beyond my means, I was extremely surprised to meet Alice at the door. She told us that she was a student there, as George paid her fees and rented accommodation in the town for her.

Everybody at our college soon knew what was going on and Alice got no sympathy, but the rumours eventually reached her home, too. Her mother came to discover the truth, because Alice had told her parents that I was paying for her and that her sister was accusing her of running off with her husband just to make her look bad in everyone's eyes. The poor mother, a simple old peasant woman, did not know what to believe, so I suggested they send her to me to hear my part at first hand – not quite first-hand because we needed an interpreter. Daudi took on this unpleasant task, when I had to confirm to the mother that Alice was telling the lies and Susan was the innocent victim in this affair. The poor old lady was deeply upset about her promising younger daughter and all the trouble in the family.

Two days later the sun was already setting on the track to college in its usual blaze of orange and gold, when I met Alice for the last time as I was coming from Iganga and she was going back there. It was a hurried meeting as her *boda-boda* was waiting.

'I am so happy to see you,' she greeted me. 'I have been to your house but I *bounced*. I need to talk to you. I have no money again, and my course is not finished.'

'But George is paying, isn't he? He is treating his family very badly because of you. I told you to stay away. You don't do what I say and then you expect me to help you.'

'I'm sorry. I ask God for forgiveness. I will be very good from now on, but I must finish my course. Then I will get a job far away and have nothing more to do with the people here.' She looked me in the eye and sounded completely plausible.

'How can I believe you when you have lied so often? What about all these stories you told your parents? Go home to your village and show that you are serious about being good. Stop seeing your brother-in-law. If you can't do that, I can't and I won't help you. I'm sorry.'

And I really was, because I thought she was only using her brother-in-law in the hope of gaining an independent future with a good job. His was the real wickedness, but she shared in the trail of unhappy relations. I did not want to be associated with this and could see no way to help her in future if she ignored everything I said. It filled me with sadness to see what I had considered a promising young lady riding off into the dusk without the slightest desire to change her ways. When I got back, I was told that she had been summoned to meet her mother and had not been to my house at all.

View from hilltop in Kinkizi

19. CHRISTMAS IN KINKIZI

Cloudless day followed cloudless day and every day was a little hotter than the last, so I was really looking forward to Christmas in the high hills near Uganda's border with Congo, where it would be cooler. Friends from Jinja had invited me to join their family in their home village for the short holiday between Christmas and New Year. Of the five members of their immediate family, the two eldest boys, teenagers, had been sent ahead by bus, so that there would be room for the rest. Even so we were packed like sardines in the double cabin pick-up. Edward, the father, drove all the way with me in the front seat and Molly, his six-year-old step-sister, wrapped round the gears between us. Behind were Joan, his wife, with their two-year-old daughter Elli, the two younger boys and Elli's nursemaid all sandwiched between bags and baggage, while the back was also fully loaded with food, bedding, bits of machinery and a couple of men.

Lengthy stops were required in the major towns en route to visit friends and relations and wish them a happy Christmas – and stretch our legs. Late in the afternoon we arrived in Kanungu, where the relations began in earnest. Joan's mother had a small restaurant in the town and Uncle Peter kept the village shop with bar attached. We did not stop for long, as it was important to get to their house before dark to set up the generator. The house was a neat brick building with a tiny kitchen, sitting and dining areas, three modest bedrooms, the main one with en suite 'bathroom', recently added by making a hole in the wall of a full-length wardrobe at floor level to let out the waste water from bathing with a basin. Behind the house were garage, kitchen and store room and next to them, up a few steps, was another house with three bedrooms and a sitting room. This had been Edward's bachelor residence and now provided sleeping quarters for the four boys and other visitors. Further away at the back were two roofed cubicles: the pit latrine and another bathroom. Two water tanks caught the rainwater from the roofs at the back.

Any extra water had to be fetched from a spring some way off. The main house was wired for light and plugs for radio and kettle. The small generator ran in the garage from dusk until ten. After that it was candles and torches.

Edward had an important and well-paid job in Jinja and Joan worked as well, so they were wealthy compared with the people living here as subsistence farmers. The land was steep yet fertile, yielding ample food crops, but remoteness and the difficulty of keeping the winding roads repaired made getting produce out to other markets a serious problem. Bananas, maize, millet, tea, coffee and all sorts of vegetables, including Irish potatoes, cabbage and carrots grew well. The surroundings were beautiful with a variety of trees, the patches of various crops interspersed with fenced grazing for cattle on the hillsides and the cool air clear like in old paintings. Chickens wandered about at will while goats were tethered all over the place.

On Christmas Eve we went to the afternoon Carol Service in the local cathedral. It was hot and sunny outside when we entered the lofty church. Not many people had arrived when the choir filed in for a practice. They were followed by a boys' brass band. As the church began to fill, a cool breeze started up and in the distance thunder rumbled. The service began, although people were still arriving. To my surprise, I didn't recognise a single carol tune, although Joan assured me that they were all English ones, brought by the early missionaries. They must have been adapted beyond recognition. The choir were very good, but the band strained the ears, as they made up in volume what they lacked in skill. It grew dark and a cold wind whipped through the church. The windows were hastily closed, while the choir chased their sheet music. Then the rain came rattling down on the iron roof almost drowning the thunder. Although it was difficult to hear anything, the service continued. By the end the storm had moved on and the congregation was invited to introduce any visitors they had brought. As a result a number of people, mostly Europeans here to enjoy a holiday in this lovely cool area, came to the front where all could see them and either they themselves or their hosts explained who they were. These introductions were an excellent idea. A few words satisfied the general curiosity and everybody clapped to welcome the stranger. Whether this is an old custom, or one that only dates from the time of insurrection, when unknown people could easily be enemies or troublemakers, I don't know, but people were still encouraged to report strangers to their LCs as a security measure. Among the foreigners were an elderly lady who sat with the clergy, a retired missionary back for a lengthy visit, and a young Norwegian volunteer who had brought her parents to see this beautiful part of the country. Many of the locals were visitors too, in that they worked elsewhere and only came back at Christmas, suddenly filling the area with doctors, health workers, teachers, business men and government officials.

After the storm it was cold outside and beginning to get dark. We went to Joan's mother's home across the road. People were still arriving from Kampala into the great party atmosphere as members of the extended family met for the first time since the previous Christmas. Swarms of children of all ages rushed about, while food was gradually served to everyone present. At first people came and talked to me, but later they got into deep conversations with their relatives and I just sat and listened. That was interesting, as often, especially when talking about their work or schools, they spoke English or a curious mixture of English and the local language. For the first time in months I felt cold – quite pleasant for a change.

Eventually people began to leave. It felt like midnight, but I think it was much earlier, when we too went home. It was too late for little stepsister Molly to go home to her mother, who lived ten minutes walk further up the track, so she slept on a mattress on the floor of my room. Her position in the family was quite strange. Edward had three brothers and four sisters. When his mother died his father married a much younger woman and had another four children with her. He died an old man, but his second family was still young. His four sons from the first marriage then each adopted one of the children from the second.

They took them to live with their own families, which was very good for the children, but left their poor mother alone and childless in the village. I found this very sad. Molly was treated exactly like the other children and seemed happy with the arrangements, though she was also delighted to see her mother again.

The local village church stood on a bluff with a magnificent view of the little fields with euphorbia hedges, maize and millet plots, banana groves, dark green velvet patches of tea bushes and the occasional fiery flowers of erythrina trees. On Christmas morning we drove there, although it was not far and the track was not suitable for a vehicle. The church itself was a modest tin-roofed building, with banana fronds decorated with bunches of flowers making an avenue to the door to mark the great feast. The pews at the front and the few benches were about half full when we arrived. Best clothes were the order of the day. It was easy to pick out the visitors, as they were very smart, especially the children: little boys in suits with waistcoats, girls in frilly dresses, all with shoes and socks. The locals were colourfully but more economically clothed: the men in long white *kanzus*, the women draped in bright wraps and the children clean and neat but barefoot.

The service appeared to begin with communion, rather surprisingly. Edward explained that this was for the regular churchgoers, who had arrived in good time. The latecomers were still pouring in and it was important that all should be present for the next part of the service. By the end of the sermon and several hymns, the church was overflowing. Then people were called up in their villages to make their offerings. Small brown envelopes were brought to the front in procession followed by a calf, three or four goats, dragged in by small boys who could hardly control them, chickens, bunches of bananas, potatoes, cabbages, eggs, beans, baskets, mats, anything that parishioners produced and could afford to give. Finding places to tie the animals was not easy, especially the frisky goats, which threatened to overthrow the altar. The vicar, a thin gentle little man in a worn cassock, prayed over the gifts, before the fun began and everything was auctioned off amid shouts and laughter. Finally, just one hen was left. The auctioneer called on individuals to bid for it. All the bids were collected until no one gave any more. In this way a great basket full of cash was gathered. Then with much merriment, the elders presented the hen to me, despite my very modest contribution. While the congregation chatted, the elders counted the money. Finally, in what was evidently the Parish Annual General Meeting, the previous year's accounts and the next year's budget were announced, together with the sum just collected which amounted to almost the entire income of the church for the whole year. Much of it had been contributed by the rich 'townee' relations – their contribution to the local subsistence economy.

We did not stop to chat in the hot noonday sun, but drove back to Edward's brother's house, a very smart new bungalow set in generous grounds next door to Edward's. We were to have lunch there together with another brother and his family. The children were all very excited to meet their cousins again and had much news to catch up on. They revelled in each other's company, as did their elders and we all enjoyed a splendid meal with goat meat cooked in different ways the main delicacy. A particularly tasty dish consisted of intriguing bits of offal in a delicious sauce, the like of which I tasted nowhere else. Each wealthy home had a brightly decorated Christmas tree and a few cards, but no presents were exchanged. The children all had new clothes, but even these did not give rise to rivalry. Everyone was very friendly, relaxed and happy.

Quite late in the afternoon we set off for further celebrations at a hotel being built at the foot of the escarpment about two thousand feet lower down on a road leading to the Congo. The large flat site was full of buildings in all stages of completion, but only a very small section was open, with a bar, a huge television screen and loud music. Tables and chairs were set out on the grass and more and more people arrived for an early evening drink – that was all this hotel could offer so far. It seemed an extraordinary spot for such a huge commercial undertaking, miles from the nearest good road, though it was near the back entrance to a famous game park. The owner said he expected it to succeed as a conference centre, but with the only reasonable access by air this seemed a pipe dream. We enjoyed our drinks in a party of twenty or more, before driving back in the moonlight.

Over the next few days we visited a number of relations and friends and one of the highlights for me was a picnic with the young people on a high hill about two hours walk to the north. The dozen youngsters aged from four to sixteen carried a large transistor radio and a crate with enough soda bottles for us all – and at times the four-year-old – up the winding track. At one point we lost it and found ourselves traversing up through thorny scrub, but it was worth it. The magnificent panorama at the top covered a huge area: from the mountains on the Congo border beyond Lake Edward to the east to Lake George and the Rwenzori Mountains just about visible to the north. In the south east the four thousand meter high extinct volcano Muhavura showed its tip between the high ranges separating us from its base, black against a thunderous sky. In the west the road could be seen winding away to Rukungiri, the district headquarters. At our feet, homesteads, schools and churches were scattered among the fields. A young man who had been clearing the bush for a new field came over to join us and pointed out his home down below. The children were very excited and danced about until it was time to go. We found the way down more easily because the path was clearly visible. Once we were back among the houses the four-year-old led us, running all the way home and not allowing Molly to pass him.

In the evening we went for a drink in Peter's bar in Kanungu, very different from the grand hotel-to-be in the plains. Eight or nine of us squeezed round a small coffee table in the shop, Joan sitting on a sack of rice, by the light of two hurricane lamps, with the talk of local politics and news of the district, which became notorious the following year after the strange religious killings reported world-wide.

More family visits and parties followed. The houses we visited ranged from very simple ones to mansions which were only occupied by their rich owners at Christmas. We also visited a women's group who had erected a hall with small rooms off as their headquarters. Having achieved this with help from Action Aid and Joan they used it for group meetings, trainings, a nursery school and cultural activities, as well as literacy and child care classes, when they could get teachers. Women came from a number of nearby villages and on this day they sang and danced for us and presented Joan with a goat and eggs from their farming projects. They also had a number of sewing machines intended for income generation, but no one had the skills to use them effectively. The people with the necessary skills – and there were plenty – did not want to live and work in such remote places, and the local women, married with large families, land and animals to maintain, could not get away for the necessary training. Anna, the leader of this group, was an enthusiastic and hard-working woman, but even she was caught in this trap, a very common one in rural areas.

The week was filled with all these new experiences for me, as well as learning how to harvest sorghum, the local grain, with a small curved reaping knife and how to pluck tea. It was with regret that we all returned to our separate work places.

20. SUSAN'S HARDSHIP

I had met three members of staff at a tutors conference before I arrived at the college. Two of them, George and Odongo, lived two and three doors from me respectively. They were cousins and not of the local tribe, like many other staff in the college housing. Both had various income generating projects running from home as they were not highly paid. George was a hearty fellow who liked a drink in good company. He had four children of his own and various relations, including Alice and Daudi lived in the house, at least during term time. He kept battery hens, so I used to get my eggs from his family. This is how I first met Susan, his wife. She seemed even smaller than she really was, as she was shy and retiring. She said so little at first that I thought she could not speak English. Always surrounded by a swarm of children she would get one of the older ones to deal with me. Often she had other visitors: students or staff members sitting outside the house which, being the end of the terrace, differed a little from the rest. With no walls around the outside for privacy it had a more open and spacious area for sitting, a favourite occupation at the end of the day.

My first real encounter with Susan was on the morning she came to ask me where I was taking her sister Alice. As she was angry and apprehensive when she arrived, my first impression was of someone filled with hate and possibly envy, but as she told the tale of her sister's treachery, my sympathy for her grew. She wanted the best for her children, just as she had wanted the best for Alice when she was small, but fate and her husband were against her. She had trained as a nurse before her marriage and had worked as such when the family first came to the college, but her husband wanted her to give up her job to look after the children and his chickens. With her career Susan lost all economic independence, becoming totally reliant on her husband for her own and the children's welfare. The youngest child was Jamie, a toddler of about one. Susan had to look after the extended family and do most of the work on the land which was allocated to lecturers for growing food crops. Now her husband wanted to get rid of her so that he could live with her young sister. As a result the house was full of tension and hate, causing the small children to fall ill frequently.

When she came to remonstrate about the removal of her sister, Susan pricked my conscience when she repeated several times, 'You are a mother, too. You must understand. I only want the best for my children.'

'Come and see me when Alice has gone, and we'll see if there is anything I can do to help,' I suggested.

She came at dusk that night, slipping in quietly at the back door.

'I can't stay. I haven't told the children where I'm going. I don't want anyone to know I have come to you,' she said. 'They'll only start talking.'

'Well, what can I do for you?'

'My husband gives me no money to feed the children. We have no sugar in the house. I want to earn a little, so that I can buy what we need.'

'What about your eggs?' I wanted to know.

'He counts all the eggs and I have to give him the money for them. Even the children are not allowed to eat any.'

I would simply take some, I thought, but I was not prepared to say it for fear of making matters worse. I had heard that he beat her, so giving him any further excuse was pointless.

'What I could do, if I had the money, is to sell some medicine to the primary student teachers. They often come to me with their health problems and they pay for their medicine, because the student clinic rarely has any.'

No doubt she had heard that I was already supplying Ruth to help her set up her clinic. I mentioned this wondering if there might not be a conflict of interest between the two of them.

'I don't think so. Ruth doesn't work here on the campus. She has her place in the village and the students don't go there.'

Tribalism probably played a part in this, too: Ruth was local and Susan came from another area; the students preferred treatment from a member of their own tribe.

'That's not a problem then,' I said. 'I have medicines here. You can make a list of what you need most and I'll let you have it. When you have sold it you can pay for a new lot. Any profit you can use for the children.'

'That's wonderful. Thank you, thank you. I'll bring the list in the morning, but I must go now.'

Next morning she came with little Jamie in tow. A bit overawed at first he soon settled happily with a drink and a biscuit, while we sorted out some basic drugs.

'I wont take them now. I'll come for them tonight,' Susan said. 'I don't want anyone to see me taking anything from your house.'

'I'll come for some eggs tonight and bring this bag,' I offered, 'then you needn't come at all.'

After that Susan came quite often usually with Jamie and sometimes with her youngest daughter as well. The children were always quiet and well-behaved. They never came on their own, but Jamie always came rushing up with a big smile to shake my hand if he met me outside. Susan continued to avoid the neighbours on her visits, coming to the front door in the mornings on her way back from the garden, when no one was about, but in the evening she would come to the back because the neighbours were sitting outside their front doors. The whole campus fed on gossip, and my activities were no doubt a favourite topic. This had its advantages, for people were always concerned and ready to help me, but I could not blame Susan for wanting to avoid extra tongue-wagging.

Susan was gentle and generous. Embarrassed if I offered her anything she always tried to repay me, often with various local delicacies to try: mushrooms, roasted groundnuts or sesame seed. When she had prepared them she brought a little dish full. This was very thoughtful, because if I didn't like it I didn't have to eat it and no offence was given. I did try everything I was offered –

except when some children catching live ants outside and scrunching them in their teeth with great delight invited me to join them. I could not face that any more than the queen termite, a soft grub the size of my thumb, presented by the young man who had dug it out of an ant hill by my house. That, too, was considered a great delicacy, so I think he was happy that I refused it.

Susan's medical practice was not a great success, as much of the medicine went to her own children. The students were not good at paying for theirs and she was too kind to insist. The college dispensary suddenly received drugs, too, and these being free for the students, they went there instead.

It gradually became clear that the affair between George and Alice was by no means over. He stayed away with increasing frequency, leaving the family without money, as he spent it all on Alice. The atmosphere seemed a little less tense than earlier. However, Susan said that her husband wanted to send her away, so that he could install her sister in the house to look after the children. This appeared a ridiculous idea. Alice was after the bright lights and a fine future well away from this college in the bush, where everyone disapproved of her. The last thing she wanted was to look after her sister's children and household, so this did not seem to be a real danger. The greater was my shock when I came back from leave to be told that a week or two before there had been the most dreadful scene, when George had finally sent his wife away. She had packed her bags and was ready to leave. At the last moment the children understood what was happening and set up such a howl that all the neighbours came running. The director and the LC1 chairman were called to arbitrate and George was told that he could not do this if he wanted to keep his job at the college. So Susan stayed and superficial calm returned. George started a postgraduate course which took him away for half of every week and this helped, too. He paid the children's fees, but left no money for their maintenance providing a constant headache for his wife. The chickens were slaughtered as they came to the end of their laying life. As they were replaced by turkeys and broilers, the latest fashion in projects, there were no more eggs.

Unable to see any future for herself in this place, Susan began to look for work which would enable her to get away and, if at all possible, take at least the two youngest children with her. She hoped to resume her nursing career but with children to care for this was not going to be easy.

In the crowd at the Cardinal's Mass every woman had a baby!

21. THE CARDINAL'S VISIT

Emmanuel, Cardinal Nsubuga, head of the Catholic Church in Uganda was to visit a near-by village. For this great occasion the college lorry was pressed into service to carry the items necessary for the celebration: a live goat and a sack of maize flour for the Cardinal, benches for seating the guests and firewood from a nearby saw mill to cook the huge bunches of green bananas also piled on the back. A number of people squeezed on, too.

The journey was quite short and the morning fine. At the parish which was our destination a raised altar stood in an open grassy space surrounded by rows upon rows of benches under awnings. Mr. Musuki, the organiser of our group, promptly disappeared, leaving me with his old mother who did not speak a word of English. We sat down on a bench at the back, but almost immediately an usher appeared and whisked me away, not allowing the old lady to come with me. I was shown to a chair in the middle of an empty front row. For ages nobody else came to sit there, as VIPs do not arrive early. When they did, I didn't know any of them and discovered later to my embarrassment that I was between the local member of parliament and his wife. We were not introduced and they were very busy talking to everyone else around them, as all these important people knew each other.

The Cardinal arrived soon after us, preceded by the same noisy boys' brass band which had played at Paul's school prize-giving. He was greeted on every side and followed by crowds. The women in these parts have a particularly shrill cry which is the equivalent of a cheer and was liberally used, also later during the service. The Cardinal, a small elderly man walking with the aid of a stick, moved slowly to buildings in the distance, where he disappeared from view.

Soon he reappeared robed for the service, which included much singing by different choirs, confirmation of numerous adults, twelve weddings and a long sermon. A thirteenth couple arrived too late for the main service and had to be married by the local bishop at the end of the long proceedings. But that was not really the end, as we all followed the Cardinal in slow, colourful procession round to the school where he laid the foundation stone for a new classroom. Fortunately this did not take very long. A quick reshuffle followed: the altar was dismantled, armchairs for the cardinal's entourage and benches for other important guests were moved under the tarpaulin in its place and a concert was about to begin. Thunder rumbled ominously, the sun disappeared into rapidly advancing black clouds and, just as the first group of school children started their welcoming song, the heavens opened with unusual generosity. The crowd scattered rapidly in search of shelter. The VIPs were all safe under the tarpaulin – or so we thought. The volume of water was such that it made pools on the tarpaulins; every little hole became a water spout and the whole roof sank lower and lower. People tried to hold it up and tip off the water, but it found the cracks between the sheets and cascaded into the audience. The Cardinal was led away under a huge striped umbrella and the rest had to fend for themselves. Most rushed for the school buildings. I had been talking to the only white man there apart from our bishop: a Polish priest who had brought the brass band. He told me to follow him. We tried the school but it was impossible to get in through the crowd at the door.

'Come on,' he said, and plunged on through the water which was now ankle deep on the ground. We reached a veranda not overflowing with people. It was the priests' house, and there in the end room the Cardinal and several VIPs sat comfortably in the dry. I felt very embarrassed, dripping as I was, soaked to the waist and therefore not keen to sit down. While I dripped quietly in a corner, the bishop came in and we talked a little. As the rain was beginning to ease, he said to the Polish priest and me: 'Come on, I'll take you to lunch. We have been asked to the M.P.'s house.'

'I can't go,' I said. 'I haven't been invited.'

'Oh, don't worry,' said the bishop, 'I'll take you in my car. It's just outside, so we won't get much wetter.'

So the three of us got into the Bishop's car. He turned the key in the ignition; nothing happened. He tried again: still nothing. Suddenly he laughed.

'Oh dear, I forgot. They borrowed the battery for the loudspeakers.'

'Never mind,' said the Polish priest, 'we can go in our bus. The boys won't mind waiting until we come back.'

The brass band boys and their instruments were turned out of the bus. We got in. Father started it up and immediately the wheels began to spin and it would not move. The boys and bystanders made valiant efforts first to push it and then to dig it out, but to no avail. In the process we were all liberally sprayed with mud. The bishop meanwhile had gone back to his little car and got the battery fixed. He drove out to the road before he asked us to join him. A couple of large ladies squeezed into the back giving extra ballast to hold us down on the skating-rink-like dirt road.

We travelled quite a distance but as the road was fairly straight and level, there was little risk of getting stuck. Passing other cars was quite nerve-wracking, but we reached our destination safely. It was a well built bungalow in an attractive compound with trees and flowers. I asked if I could possibly wash before going in, as I did not want to leave a muddy pool on and under the chair. To my amazement I was taken to an outside tap with running water in a yard at the back of the house – running water right there in the middle of nowhere. It was pumped from an underground storage to a header tank which fed several taps in and behind the house. What luxury!

The meal was excellent, but anything would have tasted good by then. It was nearly five o'clock. The company was good, too. I was wedged between a buxom police woman and her friend, who helped to keep me warm in my damp clothes. They were very friendly and chatty and hoped I would come to visit them some time. Everyone was happy and there was much laughter and even singing. The party did not last very long, however, because people had to get home before dark, or at least to a better road than the one outside. Soon farewells were said and the guests departed. The bishop offered to take me home, as he was going that way. We returned the Polish priest to his bus, which had been dug out in the meantime, and picked up two girls returning to the parish where the bishop was going to spend the night. They sat behind, so I didn't really see them, but I met both of them again later.

22. WEDDING AND AFTERMATH

The invitation was to a "Wedding Meeting" in the college staff room. I had heard that David Mwanga, one of the most popular lecturers, was getting married, but had not realised it was so soon, nor did the staff room seem a very suitable place for a Christian wedding. I did ask about it before going at the appointed time and gathered that it was not the ceremony and there was no need to dress up or take a gift, so I went along to see what it was all about.

It was a business meeting. Friends and relations had been called together to plan the financing of the wedding and pledge their help in material terms. There was a long typed list of expenses, including clothes for the bride and groom and their attendants as well as the more usual items: the service, reception, transport, photographs, invitations, service sheets and decorations. The people at the meeting were expected to supply an item or promise to pay for it, or simply to make a financial contribution, which the couple could use as they wished. In addition they were to suggest and approach friends who might be willing to contribute. A whole series of these meetings was held in good time before the wedding. Some of the details were fascinating. This wedding was to be in the capital: how could the families and friends from the village get there most economically? It was much cheaper to buy a cow locally for the refreshments, but where would the meat be roasted and how would it be transported to the reception? The couple did not come from wealthy families and while David received a salary, Clare was still a student. They had met in the city where most of their friends worked, so they wanted the wedding there rather than nearer home.

The great day came: a Saturday in August in the middle of teaching practice. The ceremony was in the cathedral, which was quite small as it had been built as a parish church for expatriates. The service had to start punctually at two because of another wedding in the church that afternoon. When I arrived at that time, the church was still empty. Gradually the guests arrived, but I recognised no-one. Eventually the bride in flowing white gown and the groom in a neat light brown suit preceded by their ballerina-like little flower girls, a smart page boy and an ample matron processed down the aisle to organ music and song. The service with the usual excellent singing was fairly short. The bridal procession left, the bridesmaids with their powder-and-lipsticked little faces almost dancing to the music. Still I did not see anyone I knew, except the groom and the college director, who had given him away – not another soul from the college. In the church I had already considered not going to the reception for this reason. I was on my way to the car when a former student stopped me and started chatting and then suddenly colleagues were everywhere. They had come in the college lorry and been held up in traffic, or started so late, that they had missed the ceremony.

Wedding group

The reception was at the university and we all made our way there. Parking was chaotic because as usual the available space was inadequate – but at least there was plenty of time. The hall was not yet open for guests, so we sat outside trying to find a bit of shade from the afternoon sun. It was all very colourful and cheerful, with photographers going round taking pictures of the splendidly dressed guests. They tried to sell the prints before the end of the afternoon. As some of the guests had not seen each other for a long time, there were emotional reunions. Finally, like children from the school playground, we were allowed into the hall festooned with gold decorations, flowers and balloons.

Between four and five hundred guests sat fairly tightly packed in long rows facing the stage where the table for the wedding party was laid. In front of it was another table with the cake – a most elaborate three-tiered affair with connected side shoots, all covered in swirls of coloured icing. The immediate families of the bride and groom sat at smaller tables at right-angles to the top table below the stage. In the corner was a table where the guests placed their gifts as they came in. Long after the guests had settled the wedding party arrived to loud music and tremendous cheers. As soon as they were seated grace was said and they were served food and bottled drinks. The guests received their refreshments in little parcels together with a bottle of soda. The food, as at most weddings, consisted of two or three bite-size pieces of roast meat, two samosas and a small cake. The drink was most welcome. After the meal came one or two speeches, before the cutting of the cake. The whole wedding party processed down to the cake table. The bride made the first cut amid tremendous cheering. She then had to give the first piece to her husband, kneeling before him to do so. Then she and her husband each took a plate to their families where again she had to kneel to present the cake. In the meantime helpers quickly cut the cake and its satellites into small pieces which were taken round to the guests. More speeches followed and a bit of singing, before the bridal party left to get changed and the guests had a chance to talk to each other, while the empties were collected.

When the bridal party returned with the bride in a smart new outfit, yet more speeches followed, in English or the vernacular, before she and the groom left with their attendants to strains of 'For they are jolly good fellows' and loud cheering. By this time the sun was setting and people were anxious to go, but with so many it took a while to get out of the hall and into the confusion of cars all trying to leave at once. This slowed things down considerably, especially when two cars collided and blocked the exit. But as so often, it was all sorted out with good humour and no tempers lost.

Some weeks later David asked me to come round to his house in town and meet Clare properly. I thought he had only asked me and took the opportunity to request his help in buying Paul's bicycle. He agreed to do this without further comment. When I went to the house I was surprised to find a number of women preparing food. David came into town with me and Paul, whom I had brought along. We settled the business, but then I had to take Paul back to my house where he had left the family bicycle. By the time I returned to David's house about twenty people had gathered and were in the middle of a meal. This was the 'after party' to thank those who had helped with the wedding arrangements, quite a formal function with speeches by most of the people present wishing the young couple well for the future. It was also a good opportunity to chat to colleagues and get to know Clare a little. She was delightful and it would have been good to have her close by, but she had to return to university so I did not see her after this.

Nearly a year later, everybody was suddenly congratulating David and he came in for a certain amount of teasing in the staff room. One day I asked him what he had done. He had become the father of twins! This was considered a great achievement, but it brought problems for the little family. Later Clare told me that her course had finished only just before the twins were due. In fact, they arrived the day after Clare's last exam. It must have been very hard, as she was in Kampala while David had a particularly busy time at college making the final arrangements for teaching practice. The twins were born in Kampala's main hospital where Clare was terrified that something would happen to them, as babies were quite often abducted and many died in the premature baby unit. She was lucky, however, and took two healthy baby girls home with her. Her course over, she was also free to come and live with her husband. He was a very caring father and helped to look after the children. There were, of course, practical problems with more than one baby: you could not carry two on your back. Travelling any distance became a major operation, as there always had to be a second person to help. A young relation did this for Clare and David during the holidays, but during term time finding such help proved difficult.

Having missed her graduation ceremony Clare had to go to Kampala to make arrangements to get her certificate and a place at the next graduation. David asked me if I could give her a lift when I was going. That seemed easy enough until we tried to fit Clare, the twins, the two girls who helped to look after them and all the things they needed, including a substantial amount of maize flour to feed them all, into my little car. In the end we had to leave one of the girls behind, but otherwise the journey went well, as did the return three days later.

The little family moved onto the campus later when David took on a different responsibility at the college. He called at my house shortly after New Year. I asked him in and then said my usual piece:

'What can I do for you?'

'I only came to wish you a happy New Year.'

That was typical of David, and a great joy to me, accustomed as I was to being asked to give something. Unfortunately even with the family near me, I saw next to nothing of them until I went to say goodbye.

23. JOE'S PERSISTENCE

At the start of the long holidays in my second year, Joe appeared. A big strong-looking lad in a light blue shirt and grey trousers, slightly baggy at the knees, he did not remove his shoes when I invited him in and sat down at the table without being asked. After the greeting he wasted no time.

'Madam, I want to work for you.'

'Why? What could you do for me?'

'I have finished Senior 4 (the GCSE class at school). I have nothing to do now. I can fetch your water and look after your garden.'

'I already have somebody for the water and I look after the garden myself so I don't need any more help. Is there no one else you could work for? What about your own family? Where do you live?'

'My father has a shop at the end of this road.'

'Why don't you help him?'

'He doesn't like me. He never helps me. He doesn't want me in his shop. Anyway he isn't very busy and he doesn't make much money. Madam, I also need money for further studies. I have no one to help me. I need a job.'

'What do you want to do for further studies?'

'I want to stay at school and do 'A' levels.'

'Will your results be good enough? What are your best subjects?'

'English, History and Divinity.'

Everyone did 'A' level History and Divinity as they were reputed to be the easiest.

'That doesn't sound very hopeful, even if you do well. Two years in the sixth form, and then what? If no one can pay your fees perhaps you should look for a shorter, more practical training. What about building, carpentry or bicycle repairs? There is plenty of that kind of work about.'

'I want work in an office.'

'Well, go away and find out what courses are available and what examination passes you need. What about the technical school here?'

'Oh no, that's no good. I don't want to go there. They don't teach you anything.'

'Well, go all the same and find out what courses they run and ask if anyone else can employ you. I'm afraid I can't.'

'Can I take your newspaper?'

'Another day. I haven't read it myself yet.'

'Can I read it here?'

'Yes, I suppose so.'

He made himself comfortable in one of the armchairs and stayed for an hour or more before he asked, 'Can I have this page?'

'Why? What is it?'

'There is a competition. You can get a mobile phone. I want that.'

'Forget it. You can't use it here. We are too far away for it to work, otherwise some of the staff here would surely have it. Don't waste money you haven't got on useless letters.'

'Alright then. I'm going. I'll be back.'

I checked Joe's story with my neighbours. Apparently he was not a bad boy and it was true that his father had no time for him. He lived with his mother and a growing number of siblings not far away, where they had some land.

Two days later Joe was back. Was I prepared to help him?

A sizable piece of land beyond the area I cultivated behind the house was still my garden. My neighbours had grown maize and later groundnuts on it, but they seemed to have lost interest. Just then it was a wilderness with waist-high weeds. Joe could clear it, grow anything he wanted and sell his crop. In this way the land would be used and Joe would have something useful to do, giving him the chance to make some money for himself. He was not enthusiastic, but agreed to have a go.

Several days later he came at about eleven o'clock and wanted a hoe to start work. Everybody else had long finished in their gardens. People did not dig in the midday heat – except Joe. He hacked away at the weeds in desultory fashion for half an hour or so, before he came to the door again.

'Give me water to drink.'

'Why have you come so late, Joe? It's hot now. Come back early tomorrow and work while it's cool.'

'I can't.'

'Why not?'

'I must dig for my mother every morning.'

'So you have land. Can't you help your mother to grow more crops so that the surplus can be sold to raise some fees for you?'

No answer.

Over the next two weeks he cleared his patch slowly. I had a compost heap and asked him to put the weeds on it, explaining the benefits of this, but he continued to leave them where they had fallen. When he had cleared about half the area he came in again.

'Madam, I am ready to plant now. Give me some seeds.'

'What do you want to plant?'

'Tomatoes.'

'Isn't that too difficult? They need a lot of care: watering, fertiliser and pesticides, so I am told. Can you manage all that?'

'Hm, I don't know.... You give me some maize seed.'

'I haven't any. But I tell you what you could do: you could plant beans with the maize. I have just seen this method demonstrated at a plant nursery in Iganga. Why don't you try it? You put in the maize seeds in the middle and three or four beans around the outside. The beans help the maize to grow and the maize supports the bean plants.'

'Alright. I'll try it. But I have no seeds.'

'Don't you have maize and beans at home?'

'Not for sowing. Only for eating. I need money to buy seeds.'

Although I didn't believe this, I gave him some money. He duly returned with two little paper parcels, one of maize corns and one of beans. He planted them in alternate rows, not as I had suggested. Did he not understand or was he unwilling?

He came almost every day and he always wanted something: money for this or that, sugar, the boots I used for gardening, old newspapers to sell, a pen, an envelope, a stamp, my radio when I went away for the weekend. Could he come in to read the newspaper? It was annoying always having to say 'no'. I began to dread his visits. He often lay in wait for me when I came back after the weekend. It became quite unnerving.

One Saturday night when I had come home late to find the electricity off, he knocked at about nine o'clock, well after dark. I only opened the door a crack.

'May I come in?'

'No. What on earth do you want now?'

'Please, Madam, I am sick. Help me. I need medicine. I've got herpes. It's terrible. Shall I show you?' His hand went to the waistband of his trousers.

'No thank you! I don't want to see you at all at this hour. I have no medicine anyway.'

'I need to go to the doctor and I have no money.'

'Well, you can't go to the doctor now, that's for sure. Come back at a sensible time tomorrow and we'll see. Good night.'

A sensible time turned out to be seven o'clock on Sunday morning. His knocking woke me, but as I couldn't see who was there I had to get up, which did not please me.

'Good morning, Madam. The money for the doctor. You promised.'

'I did nothing of the sort,' I muttered darkly. 'Can't you leave me in peace even on a Sunday?'

'I thought you would be going for prayers.... Sorry, Madam.'

I gave in, as usual.

Two days later he was back, saying he had seen the doctor who diagnosed high blood pressure and recommended a course of expensive treatment. Young people do not suffer from high blood pressure, I thought, though I may have been wrong there. I sent him to the health centre where he could get free medicine and see the visiting *muzungu* doctor on a Thursday. Moreover, he was never to knock if my curtains were drawn and under no circumstances was he to come after dark. On his next visit he reported that he had paid all the money I had given him to see the doctor at the health centre. This meant he was either very naive and had been cheated, or he was telling stories. The last seemed most likely. When no more cash was forthcoming he recovered quickly and suffered no further illness.

We then discussed at length what he could do. We went to Iganga to look at a computer school, but the course was expensive and I had serious doubts about the qualifications it promised after two years. Technical school seemed to be the answer. There was the local one, but Joe said it was very bad and he wanted somewhere that would give him 'a better chance', while I was not keen to have him on my doorstep all the time. We settled on the technical college in Iganga and I agreed to pay his fees if he could get a place. When his results came out they were not good and he had failed maths, so I was very surprised when he appeared with an acceptance slip from the Iganga Technical College: they had admitted him to the carpentry course. I agreed to pay the fees but refused to be responsible for clothing and extras, as they were his parents' responsibility.

Joe's maize was growing by now, but not as well as my neighbours'. He had used poor seed, they told me. The beans had been eaten by chickens, so he wanted to replant. Again he needed money while I wanted to know what he had done with the seeds left over from the last planting.

'Oh, my brother planted those,' he told me.

'Well, get your brother give you some more.'

This was not possible, of course, so once again I paid up, but asked him to weed the path around my house in return. For various reasons it was very difficult for him to find time for this and again he came in the heat of the day. His first act was to pull up a pretty ground-covering weed with bright red flowers, which I was encouraging to spread on the path behind the house to prevent erosion. I had specifically asked him to do nothing in this area, but when I came home after a class the damage was done. He huffed and puffed a great deal, did very little and then had to go home because it was too hot. About two hours' work took him nearly a week and he had hoed the path too deeply and left all the weeds lying there. It was such a mess of loose soil and dead plants that he would not even ride his bicycle through it. Tidying it took two more days with yet more huffing and puffing.

He always asked solicitously if I had enough water, knowing full well that the answer was 'yes'. One day I actually ran short while doing the washing and asked him if he could quickly get me a jerry can full.

'Yes, yes. I will. But I must go home and change first. I can't go like this in my dirty clothes.'

Ten minutes later he was back with shoes instead of flip-flops and a shirt instead of his ragged T-shirt. As it was late morning he was unlikely to meet anyone on the way or at the borehole.

Later when he harvested the maize, he left the stalks lying around. I asked him to burn them. He did this while I was out and burnt the hedge as well, still leaving a pile of stalks lying about. I never thought I would have to tell an African how to deal with fire, but I stood over him when I made him burn the rest.

After the maize Joe planted sweet potatoes, which are grown on little mounds. They were due to be ready before I left, because it was doubtful whether he would be allowed to go on using the land once I was no longer there. Who would look after his crops when he had to go back to college? He had enough brothers and sisters and, when it became clear that I was not going to do it, he asked one of them. I expected peace at last, but after about three weeks, who should be on the door step again but Joe?

'May I come in?'

'Sure. Sit down.'

He made himself comfortable in the armchair.

'Madam, I am having a hard time at college.'

'Why? What's the problem now?'

'I don't have a bed.'

'What have you been sleeping on for the last three weeks?'

'I used a friend's. He did not come back because he had no fees. Now he has come and he wants his bed.'

'Doesn't the college provide the beds?'

'They have some but you have to hire them. It costs too much.'

I suspected my friend of wanting cash for some other purpose, so I said I would call in at the college to settle the matter. What he had told me was correct. The best thing I could do was pay the college to buy him a bed. He received it quite quickly, but never mentioned it until I asked. He 'needed' many other things as well: tools, especially my hammer, books, trousers, shoes – even his photo taken beside my car.

Joe and my car as requested

I asked him repeatedly how he would get on if he had to depend on his family.

'But you are my mother,' he would say.

'I am not!' I assured him, muttering 'thank God!' to myself.

His mother, a surprisingly young and pleasant woman, came twice to thank me most profusely for what I was doing for Joe. As we were walking up the garden path on the second occasion, she looked at Joe's potatoes.

'They're not very good,' she said. 'They wont be ready before you go.'

'Well, it's bad luck that it's been so dry,' I replied.

'But he planted the wrong sort of potatoes. They would be much better, even with no rain, if he had planted the right kind.'

'Didn't he ask you?'

'Joe? He always knows everything better.'

The last straw was the business of his identity card. Just before the beginning of term he had apparently left this vital document in a coat which his brother had taken to Jinja where he worked. As he needed it when he went back to college, he wanted to go to Jinja to get it.

'That will be very expensive,' I said, knowing full well that I would be expected to pay the fares. 'Why don't you write to him and ask him to send it to you at college?'

'That's too dangerous. I might not get it.'

'He could send it by registered mail. It would still be much cheaper than going. I'll give you an envelope and paper. You can write it now and I'll post it in Jinja when I go.'

'You are going to Jinja?' The boy was not slow! 'Can't I come with you?'

'You can, certainly, but I won't be coming back that day. I'm not sure when I'm coming home.'

'That doesn't matter. I'll come.'

And he did.

On the way I berated him about his constant begging. Then we came through the next village, where in a very nasty incident the week before, a crowd had burnt a man to death because they thought he was a thief. The one policeman in the village had tried to arrest him, but the crowd had threatened the policeman who immediately sent for reinforcements. Even the larger police contingent had been intimidated by the crowd. It was the most savage incident I had heard of in the area and I was horrified when Joe pointed out a spot at the roadside.

'That's where we burned the criminal,' he announced proudly.

'We? What do you mean? Were you there?'

'Yes. I was helping to beat and burn him. He was a bad man.'

'How do you know? What did he do to you? Why didn't you leave it to the police to sort out?'

'He was a thief. He was a wicked man. Such people need to be punished.'

'By you? You call yourself a Christian and you help to murder a man?'

'It was not murder. He deserved it.'

'That is for the police and the court to work out. What you have done is to behave like a savage. Anyway, what were you doing in the village in the middle of the night, when you told me a few months ago that you could not come here to work because it was too far away?'

There was no answer.

When I dropped Joe off on the outskirts of Jinja, he said: 'Where is the money to get to my brother's house? And what about my fare home?'

'You insisted on coming and I have no plans to give you any more money. Sorry. Your brother will be able to help you as he is working.'

I shut the car door and drove off.

Whenever Joe went off to college, I heaved a sigh of relief, but the relief never lasted, as he turned up every few weeks. One day he met me as I was going back to the house. In the front garden a beautiful cockerel was tied to the banana tree. I was surprised, but then saw a note on the door.

'Who gave you that?' Joe wanted to know.

'It's a gift from Martha to thank me for helping her.' Martha had been one of his classmates who had also come for assistance.

'Oh.'

When my final departure approached he came again unexpectedly before the end of his term, this time bearing a large pawpaw – just as my own were ripening. It was the only gift he ever brought. Had he learned something?

'Madam, I must talk with you.'

'You may come in and sit down.'

As usual he settled himself comfortably before he started.

'Madam, you are going to England, aren't you?'

'Yes. I am going back to my family soon.'

'Madam, take me with you. I want to study there.'

'Joe, have you any idea what you are asking? I can hardly afford for you to study here; how do you expect me to do it there? Everything is much, much more expensive. It's cold there. You would not know anyone. You wouldn't like living in England.'

'Oh, but I would. I don't mind cold. I can make friends. If you can't afford for me to study, then I will work for you. (I could not imagine a worse prospect.) You must take me. You are my mother. I'll get a much better job after I've been in England.'

'Maybe, Joe. But I'm not even paying my own fare home. It costs a lot of money. How do you expect me to pay for you?'

'But, Madam, you can't just leave me here. There must be some way I could go to college there. You really must take me.'

'Forget it, Joe. If I took anybody it certainly would not be you.... If you work very hard at college and become an expert carpenter, you may be able to get a scholarship for further studies, or perhaps you could afford to come for a holiday. We would be happy to have you as a visitor for a week.'

Joe came several more times to say goodbye. He never mentioned going to England again, but he made sure he collected everything I could give him, especially the promised hammer.

More letters have come from Joe than from anyone else, with the most ingenious reasons why I must urgently send my poor son some money! He is doing quite well on the course, and I am sure he will become a rich man, even without my further assistance.

24. ENCOUNTERS WITH THE POLICE

Numerous police posts alongside main roads were intended to ensure security and safety on the roads. Those in towns were easily recognised by the number of wrecked vehicles assembled in front of them. Police often stopped drivers for overloading, excessive speed or evident mechanical defects, which could be very noticeable like the lorry I once found myself behind which had a rear wheel missing. At certain points there were regular checks and searches, particularly at the Nile crossing at Jinja unavoidable by road transport as no other bridges existed. I soon came to expect to be waved on at all these stops as an unlikely candidate for illicit activities, so being stopped was rare and disconcerting.

The first time a policeman pulled me over, he merely wanted a lift to an isolated police post further along the road. Another time I had to stop at almost the same spot, but this time the policeman inspected the outside of the car carefully before asking me for my licence. I gave him the photo-copy of my English licence which I carried. He retired behind the car with it and just as I was beginning to wonder what he could be doing with it he reappeared at the window.

'Your licence is out of date,' he said.

'That's impossible,' I replied, realising at once that he was angling for a backhander. 'Our licences are valid until we are seventy – and I wont be that old for a while. What have you found?'

He showed me where somewhere among the inside folds the words 'date of last licence' were followed by 'March 1978'. I laughed, explained and asked him if he seriously thought that I had been using an out-of date licence for the last twenty years. He apologised and let me go.

The next policeman who wanted to see my licence was more persistent. On a Sunday afternoon I was taking three children to the zoo in Entebbe when the small saloon car in front of me was pulled over by a lone policeman. As soon as he spotted me he let the other car go, stopped me and asked for my licence. I was slightly worried as I had tried to collect my Uganda licence two days before after waiting for it for many months. The revenue office had just closed so I still only had my English licence. The photo-copy was not good enough for this man..

'You can't use a photo-copy. Where is the original?'
'In my house a hundred miles from here.'
'This is illegal.'
'Are you sure? I don't think that's right.'
'You are committing an offence.'
'I don't think so.'
'You must pay a fine.'
'I don't think so.'
'I will have to take you to the police station.'
'I think you will. I am sure that it is not necessary to carry the original licence. What would I do if it was stolen? It would be difficult to get a new one from England.'
'You must go to the police station. They will fine you.'
'Where is your station?' I asked.
'Where are you going?' he countered.
'We want to go to the zoo.'
'Who are these children?'
'They belong to my friend.'
'O.K. You can go.'

The next encounter was rather more serious. My husband was visiting and had left me at a meeting on the outskirts of Kampala while he went on into town. When the meeting finished at the agreed time there was no sign of him. I started to walk and with passing time became increasingly concerned as he was always punctual. I imagined various disasters that could have happened. Finally he appeared, both he and the car in good condition. He had been stopped by a group of police officers, only because they had nothing else to do at a usually very busy spot. My road tax was out of date. David explained that it was my car so not his responsibility, that nothing could be done without me and I was waiting for him to collect me. One of them, a woman, took his driving licence off him and told him to report back with me. When we did this, the policewoman got into our car and directed us to the near-by police station where she handed us over to the man in charge. We waited and waited for something to happen. After more than an hour a youngish officer took a statement and finally told us he would have to charge me. We would have to go to the magistrates court to be fined. It was after four o'clock on a Friday afternoon. I asked him when we would have to go and to give me some idea of what the fine would be, as we had little money with us and no chance to get more without going back to the bank in Iganga which was closed until Monday. The prospect for the weekend began to look bleak. Much to our surprise the officer told us that the court was still open and would be able to deal with the matter. When he saw our genuine concern and I assured him that I had no intentions of defrauding the Uganda government he began to ask me about my work. On learning that I was a volunteer helping his country, he suddenly said,

'O.K. We'll proceed no further. I'll let you go this time, but make sure you pay your tax on Monday.'

We thanked him profusely and, enormously relieved, drove home.

When I looked out the papers for the tax renewal I was stunned to discover that it had not expired a few days but over three months earlier – a genuine mistake which I could not explain. When someone later told me what the fine for non-payment of road tax was, I felt even more grateful to the kind police officer who had let us go.

The police did not have an easy task, especially as most people were afraid of them. They usually operated in pairs to reduce the temptation to accept bribes, which was strictly forbidden, though still widely practised. I found that they spoke good English, which was the sign of some education, and they were always pleasant and courteous.

25. THE SWALLOWS

African Striped Swallows, pretty little birds with black and white speckled breasts, rusty brown heads, dark blue wings and odd blunt beaks, appeared in February and began building. They worked in pairs to construct elaborate nests in corners in or outside buildings. One pair worked just outside my garden door, but it was easier to watch the two pairs in the English classroom which was also used for Mass for the Catholic students on Sundays. This was the best time to watch them – during the second sermon which was in the local language.

Two swallows swooped in one behind the other. Oblivious of the crowded room and not in the least disturbed by the hearty singing accompanied by drums and shakers, the first one flew straight to the nest to stick on the bit of mud in its beak, while the other sat on the top of the blackboard, apparently listening attentively. The plasterer then glided round the room while his mate attached her mud. Then, with a quick twitter which sounded just like 'Come along!' they flew out. The length of time before their return depended on the weather. If it had not rained recently they might have to go some distance to find the wet mud they needed. The building was a slow and arduous business, as the nests were quite large and took several weeks to complete. When a nest was knocked down, as they often were by people who did not want the mess which later accrued underneath, the little birds just started all over again; they never gave up. They worked together in delightful harmony – a wonderful example of perseverance and team work.

I stopped workmen from knocking down the nest by my house and eventually it was finished. I could hear the pair of occupants making soft cooing noises in the evening. I looked forward to the time when there would be babies, but it was not to be. Some mysterious disaster occurred. On several occasions at around eleven o'clock in the morning about a dozen swallows would suddenly appear and fly around the nest in noisy agitation, though not one of them went in. I suspected that the lizards which lived all over the house took the eggs and perhaps even stayed in the nest, but I never saw anything go in or come out. It was charming how the other swallows came to chase away the intruders or do whatever they did to help their friends. Some months later I saw an endless row of swallows sitting densely packed on the telephone line in a swamp and then suddenly they all disappeared. The nest remained, inhabited by other birds for a while, but they too failed to breed and left, perhaps for that reason. The swallows came back briefly the next year, before someone destroyed the nest while I was away.

26. MARTHA'S TRAINING

Martha came to me at about the same time as Joe. She was from the same school, but her claim to my acquaintance rested on the fact that she had been a passenger in the back of the bishop's car, when he had brought me home more than a year earlier. A tall athletic girl with short natural hair, she wore a green blouse and faded black skirt. She hesitated about coming in and tried to go down on her knees to greet me. Like so many others she wanted to work for me and live with me. She looked like a competent worker, but as usual I told her that I did not need any help and preferred to live alone. She tugged at her skirt nervously.

'What can I do then?' she asked. 'I can't just sit and do nothing for the next three months. And when I get my results I'll have to do something and I don't know what. My family is poor. They can't afford to send me to college.'

'Well, come along in, sit down and let's think about this. Would you like a cup of tea or some juice?'

'No, thank you please. Water.'

Settled with her glass of water and some biscuits, she began to relax.

'What sort of work would you like to do? What about a dress-making course at the local technical school?' I asked.

'Oh no, not sewing. I don't like it. I would like something else.... nursing or teaching? But for that you have to train and training costs money and I don't have money.'

'How did you manage to get through school then? Who paid for that?'

'A Father from the mission paid until last year. He has gone back to Europe now. He has not sent any more money. We really struggled for the fees for this year. My father is an invalid and cannot work, so there is no money. I must find a way to earn some.'

'You need to find a suitable training place, then we'll see about paying. Now go and ask at the mission hospital what the requirements for nursing are and where you can train. You could also call in at the primary teachers college and find out if they can take you. They say that you need 'A' levels to get into teacher training, but it's a new requirement, and I think they are still taking people without.'

'All right, I'll do that. But what about now?'

'See if you can find someone who needs help, perhaps a shopkeeper in town. Then you could earn a little money.'

'I doubt if anyone will pay me. Nobody has money.'

'Well, see if you can get an unpaid job. It will be useful experience and it will look good on your CV, you know, the list of things you have done which they ask for when you apply for a place. Try the shops in town.'

'But that's difficult. How can I get to town? It's a long walk from home.'

'Didn't you walk to school every day?'

'Yes, but it was very hard. I was very tired by the time I got there. That's why my results won't be very good. It would be O.K. if I could use the bicycle, but my brother needs it. Oh well, I'll see if I can manage to get a job.'

'Good. Let's see how you get on.'

Martha came back a couple of weeks later. She had tried several people in the town, but they had been unable to offer her any useful experience. The only hope was a shop on the road near her home in the bush. It served the villagers, but it was expensive for them and she suspected not much business was done there as the people round about just had no money. Anyway, she would ask but she wanted me to come with her and have a look at the place. She also wanted me to meet her family. I agreed to do this on a Sunday morning, if she came to show me the way. Although the country is officially Christian and a very large number of people are practising church-going Christians and offices are closed on Sundays, it is otherwise business as usual, especially after noon.

I was surprised how far from the town we had to go before we reached the turn-off, just a track, to Martha's home. The shop she had mentioned was at the corner. It was a tiny place with a wide range of goods: toothpaste, little oil lamps made from old tins, hand-made rope, strips of bicycle inner tube used for tying on loads, sugar, salt and rice, plastic cups and plates, matches, aspro, cigarettes sold singly, socks, everything higgledy-piggeldy on the shelves. The owner was out but his wife and son listened to Martha and did not turn her away. Lots of dirty children crowded round, but were quickly chased out of the shop. While we were still talking, the boss came back. After some further discussion, he agreed that Martha could help him, but that he might not be able to pay her anything. Business was not good. It was the end of the dry season so no one had any money and when they did have some, more people were going to the town to get things because they were cheaper there. But yes, she could come and help.

Finally we set off on the track to Martha's home. At first it was clearly used by vehicles from time to time, but as we went further it deteriorated. At one point it became so badly rutted that I wanted to leave the car and walk.

'You can't do that,' Martha said. 'It wouldn't be safe.'

In any case I wasn't keen on a walk of indeterminate length in the midday sun. So we soldiered on and it was not actually much further. There were several houses in a largish compound. The one she took me to was furnished with a small table, one proper chair, a bench and two rickety folding chairs, but there was a clean embroidered cloth on the table. Behind the chair and the bench a piece of patterned material was draped from floor to ceiling. Through a gap I could see that raw cotton was stored behind the curtain and when I peeped through the hanging behind me there was more, so this building was probably the strongest and driest, used to store their cash crop. Father, a large elderly man wearing a *kanzu,* the long white robe traditionally worn over trousers on special occasions, and Mother, thin even in her well-worn *busuti,* came in to shake hands. Father spoke a little English, but Mother none, so she withdrew again immediately after the greeting. Other people including children just came to the door to have a look. One of Martha's brothers was introduced and he spoke reasonable English. He was a primary teacher in another village but came home at weekends to see his wife and baby and to work on the house he was building.

Martha showed me round the compound, especially the well. The water was some way down and had to be brought up and over a concrete rim at the top which was beginning to break up. It had a cover which was taken off before the water was hauled up in a battered piece of jerry can which did not hold much.

'You get very little water up with your poor container. Can't you use a bucket?' I asked, as this method seemed most inefficient.

'Its hard to get the can out over the edge. The concrete is rough and damages it and we have to keep getting new jerry cans. They're expensive, so we can't afford it,' Martha explained.

The compound was dry, dusty earth and the whole area looked over-cultivated and unproductive. One or two pawpaw trees had been planted near the houses and ducks and chickens wandered about. There was a wood pile under a big *muvule* tree, which also provided a pleasant patch of shade. Several small houses stood dotted about and Martha pointed out who lived in each. While we were walking round, Mother had made some tea. This was also a sign of poverty or the distance from shops, because normally on these occasions one was offered soda, hastily purchased from the nearest trader. I drank the tea with Martha's father in the cotton house. It was not clear how the people in the compound made a living. Martha had said that her father was an invalid, but it was not obvious what was the matter with him. They had grown some cotton, but getting it to the ginnery was a problem. It could only be taken in small quantities by bicycle, and there was only one bicycle which her brother used during the week. Yet when I left, the family insisted on giving me a large pineapple. It seemed all wrong to take something from these people but to refuse would have been a grave insult.

It was several weeks before Martha came again. She had been working in the shop and she had learned something about trading, but it would soon be over as the owner was moving his shop to the town.

'Could you not take over the shop? After all people will have to go further if there is no shop there any more. Would it not be a big help if the shop could stay open?' I suggested, thinking that she could provide a useful service to the local people.

'What would I sell?'

'The same as now. Perhaps I can help you buy the owner's stock.'

'I don't think it's possible. I'd have to live there or people would come and steal everything. I'd also need the local chief to agree and I don't think he would like a girl like me running a shop. Not enough people might come to buy. The old owner will want to keep his customers. They'll go to him in town. We could try, but I really don't think it will work.'

There would be other problems, too: how to keep the shop stocked without transport; help, as one person alone could hardly keep a shop open all the time. So we abandoned that idea.

The exam results were due soon and it was time to plot the next move. In theory students were supposed to have 'A' Levels to get into primary teacher training, but with the likely absence of enough qualified candidates, Martha could try for entry into the college in Iganga, as rumour had it that the one in our town was closing. I took her to Iganga but did not go to the college with her. She was given application forms to fill in which did not specify the entry requirements. To register a substantial fee was required which we paid. I was very angry when I learnt later that the college only accepted students with 'A' and very good 'O' Levels, but they did not tell applicants, so they collected a tidy sum from application fees of candidates who had no hope of getting a place. Every one seemed to be out to rob the poorest.

The critical subjects were mathematics and English. When the results came out, Martha had a credit in English but she had failed maths.

'Could you do better if you did it again, if you had some help?' I wanted to know.

'I honestly don't think so,' she said. 'I just can't do maths.'

Unfortunately this sentiment was very common, as maths teaching generally was sub-standard, so she was probably right.

'Try the local college,' I suggested.

She did, but without maths they did not want her either. Stalemate. Martha went home.

Two weeks later she was back. One of the sisters from the mission had taken her to a well-known primary teachers college in Kampala from which government aid had recently been withdrawn. They offered her a place, as the college was hoping to become independent if their appeal to stay as a government institution failed. It was considerably more expensive than the local one with the additional cost of travel. Since Martha had proved herself honest and a hard worker, I really wanted her to train so that she could keep herself and help her family. I agreed to take her there and hoped that I could manage to find the fees. I had a long talk with the principal, who was full of hope that their government subsidy would be restored. This would halve the fees. I felt we had little choice, so Martha started there.

Not long after this, I heard in the staff room that a student had been admitted to the local college without maths. What a fool I had been! *I* should have gone and negotiated a place for Martha instead of leaving it to her. They were unlikely to refuse me. And so it turned out. I did not even have to see the principal. In the office they told me that there was no problem about transferring a student from another college as long as she came with her papers and a good report. So at the end of the first term Martha transferred to the local college, though not without difficulty. The Kampala college at first refused to let her take away her bed and other things she had left for the holidays because they were annoyed that she was not coming back. Her father had to go and remonstrate with them, before they released her property.

One day I came home to find a very handsome cockerel tied to my banana tree, and a note on the door to say it was from her father. Joe was with me when I found it and he was impressed. I think it had never occurred to him that he could do something like that. I put the cockerel in the garage, intending to take it to my friends in Kampala a few days later. I fed and watered it, but was nearly driven demented by its crowing early in the morning. The night before I was going, I thought I would tie it up when it was dark. I knew from keeping hens for many years, that they are completely docile in the dark. Not so this cock. It was almost impossible to catch him and as it was already nearly midnight I was worried about waking the neighbours. In the end I succeeded and tied its legs together with banana fibre as Martha had done. Next morning I opened the garage door and he was sitting peacefully on a sack. I put my things in the car and got a newspaper to put him on. When I came back he had gone. There he was walking round the house, trailing the banana fibre which had worked loose. I tried to drive him back into the garage but it was hopeless. In the end I lost sight of him altogether. There was nothing for it but to tell one of the neighbours to keep an eye open for him as I had to go. He turned up at the neighbours' at dusk and they kept him for me. In the end he became a wedding present for Rachel.

Martha settled well at her new college and made good progress. She became one of their sports stars, as I heard from a colleague who taught the sports there as well. When it was time for her to go on teaching practice, not long after the beginning of a new term, she sent a message that she urgently needed money for folders, card, paper and some more items which I could not decipher. I went to the college to find out what all this was about. The sentry box at the gate was empty and I began to wonder how I would find Martha on the rambling campus, when I noticed a number of people sitting in a grass roofed hut not far away. This was the staff room. The teachers there soon sent someone to find Martha.

She nearly fell on her knees again when she saw me.

'Do tell me what all this note is about. I have brought you some paper, a couple of folders and some marker pens but I haven't any box files, and what are these other things?'

'*Manillas* and polythene papers.'

Manillas I knew were sheets of coloured card. The polythene papers turned out to plastic document wallets.

'Why do you need these things? They weren't on the list of things required for this term, were they?'

'No. But we need them for teaching practice next week.'

'What happens if you can't get them? Surely the college can help you,' I said, thinking how impossible it would be for her to buy these things if she had to get the money from home.

'Oh no. They send you away. You can't do your teaching practice unless you have all these things. Some students have gone already.'

'But how will you get the things even if I give you the money. Can you get them in Iganga or do you have to go to Jinja?'

'You can get them all here in the town. There is a shop.'

What an unfair and inefficient way to treat poor students!

The teaching practice finished just before I was leaving and Martha had done very well. She had gone to her brother's school because she could stay with him and save the cost of accommodation, and she was delighted when the head had offered to employ her at the end of her course. She was anxious that I should pay her family another visit. This time it was all much more formal and the whole family were present in their Sunday best: parents, three brothers, all introduced by name, the wives of two of them and some of their children, one a tiny baby, and finally Martha's three younger sisters, whose names I never discovered. They were only allowed to greet me on their knees before they had to disappear again to prepare food. A little later they served an excellent meal in the cotton house. This time Martha was allowed to stay and eat with us, but her mother again only made a brief appearance with the dishes. Afterwards her brothers and an uncle who spoke good English made speeches to which I had to reply. This took quite a long time. Finally there was a photo session under the *muvule* tree for all, including the severely brain-damaged little son of one of the brothers, but not her sisters. They sat to one side: whether they were too shy or not allowed to sit with the rest I don't know, but in the end they let me to take a picture just of the three of them. The whole family was so grateful and happy that Martha's future looked bright now. It was lovely to leave them all so cheerful and encouraged.

In the car on the way back to town, I asked Martha about the little handicapped boy. He was blind and unable to walk, but he had seemed well-cared for at home, where he sat on the ground under the *muvule* tree. When he cried one of the girls picked him up and comforted him. His father brought him gently cradled in his arms for the photo for which some one had dressed him in brightly patterned shorts in addition to his T-shirt. What was the matter with him? Had he ever been seen by a doctor? Could anything be done for him?

Martha's family

'He was born like that. Oh yes, they took him to the doctor at the big hospital, but there is nothing they can do. Perhaps he could get a bit better in a special school, but we can't pay for that. He is no trouble.'

They accepted this burden, along with all their others, and just coped.

Martha turned up in her maroon and yellow college uniform early on my last morning to collect various things I was leaving her: dictionary, sheets, a few clothes, paper and scraps useful for making visual aids for school. She was a great help with the final tidying and cleaning up that had to be done. The car was so full in the end that it was impossible to fit her in and my last view of her was struggling along the road under a load of bags and boxes.

27. RUKUNGIRI CHRISTMAS

Planning for my last Christmas and the Millennium was not easy. It was term time for the primary teachers, and no one, from the director down, was prepared to say which days would be holidays. My guess was that no work would be done between Christmas and New Year, but in my first year the students had done exams in that week, so I dared not risk arranging to be away. Matters were further complicated by the possibility that our eldest daughter might bring her wedding forward from May to January. For once I really felt distressed that letters from my family took three weeks, though mine often arrived in less than a week. I tried to phone home from Kampala, but failed to get a reply, so I was very unsettled. I dreamed of going back to the cool hills of Kinkizi, where I had spent the previous Christmas, but with my friends out of the country, it was not feasible. In the end chance, in the shape of the Stephen, chairman of the Rukungiri District Council, resolved the problem. We had never met before he was sent to visit me at college by a mutual friend, but when he heard how much I liked his part of the world, he invited me to spend Christmas there with his family.

On the Sunday morning of the planned departure from Kampala almost a week before Christmas, I waited and waited. We had no means of contacting Stephen and in mid-morning decided to go to church. On the way we met Stephen and his wife Margaret, full of apologies, their car overflowing.

'My nephew died yesterday,' Stephen explained. 'We have to go home for the funeral today, but Margaret has to come back to Kampala for work. You can travel with her on Christmas Eve, if you don't mind waiting.'

This meant that I would have to go back to college and teach for another two days, which salved my conscience, but the extra hundred miles of travel it involved were nothing compared with Margaret's round trip of more than four hundred miles and almost two whole days on the road.

On Christmas Eve we finally left Kampala late in the morning in a Pajero packed with Margaret's daughter Hilda and two of her school friends, Margaret's three-year-old granddaughter, Moreen, her nurse, and all the luggage, for which there was not much room. Margaret allowed me to share the driving – a help to both of us. We stopped for a quick late lunch in Mbarara.

Leaving the tarmac at Bushenyi, we took a fairly good murram road into the hills. After a further two hours contouring round beautiful cultivated hillsides, we arrived in Rukungiri, the district capital, a small town scattered on steepish slopes. We stopped only briefly for Margaret to contact some relatives before going another six miles to the family home. This comfortable three bedroom bungalow had a lawn, flower beds and a hedge in front while behind was a yard surrounded by servants quarters, stores and domestic offices. The tap on the large rainwater tank was locked, but there was running water in the kitchen and bathroom of the house. Beyond the surrounding hedge were banana plantations interspersed with other fruit trees and vegetables, all green and lush in the fertile black soil.

While the girls settled in and Moreen took me off to look at their cows in a nearby field, Margaret prepared a meal and started the generator, so the light went on when it became too dark to see. Stephen came home at dusk and we all ate together. Then the Christmas tree and decorations were put up, all very western, as both Stephen and Margaret had spent time in Britain and the United States, but even here no presents were exchanged.

On Christmas morning everybody dressed in their best clothes and we set off for an old mission station some miles away. The church was overflowing and the service well under way by the time we arrived, but seats had been reserved near the altar; at any rate, people made room for us on the few benches. Every one else stood or sat on the floor. The service seemed endless. A large number of babies were baptised, their mothers and sponsors so densely crowded round the altar that it was impossible to see anything. When they returned to their places, I watched a small girl sitting on the altar steps drumming on the floor in time to all the hymns. At the end of the service, the local politicians, Stephen and the Member of Parliament for the area, made speeches. This unusually large gathering of people from all over the district proved too good a publicity opportunity to miss, but here no Christmas offerings in kind were brought.

When we finally emerged into the sunlight outside, there was much joyful chatter. Eventually we drove home and then to lunch with the family of one of Stephen's brothers. No great celebrations took place because of the recent deaths of two family members, so it was just a big meal with various dishes, especially goat in two or three different forms – the festive speciality. The men and important women ate in the sitting room, served by women and children, who had their meal in the kitchen or outside, sitting on the ground. Some of us then walked back which was much quicker than driving, because we only had to go down into the valley and up the other side, while the track contoured through endless banana plantations.

The next day we went to the small Catholic church almost next to the house to a service conducted by a catechist. Even here priests were in short supply and this little church did not have one. As this was the Christmas service for the local people they brought their humble offerings at the end: small bags of beans and maize, three or four eggs, a cabbage. The area had suffered a severe drought earlier in the year bringing food shortages to a normally well-supplied people. Stephen said that nearly all the maize had been taken from one of his fields, but he did not mind very much, because his family had enough to eat and those who took it probably did not. He proudly showed me his farm, which was quite scattered, with fields for cattle and the banana plantation near the house; coffee and cabbages grew further away. In the valley bottom he had built drainage works and a fish pond, which was not yet fully operational. His agricultural training was put to good use on the farm and on those of his brothers.

During the next few days we went to two weddings and visited more relations. The first wedding was in the town. Timing was chaotic as so often in Uganda and we arrived at the church at the very end of the service, in time for the lengthy photo session which followed on the church steps. The clothes were similar to those worn in Kampala, reminiscent of a pageant or carnival in their flamboyance. The reception at the bride's home afterwards included an additional ceremony for another family member who had married a few months earlier. According to local custom, the bride remains at home and does nothing strenuous for the first four months of her marriage. Then a special rite takes place during which she receives gifts for her household and becomes a full working member of it. The presents ranged from cows and goats to blankets and kitchen utensils, each item proclaimed by the master of ceremonies together with the donor's name and relationship. The wedding reception included no such formal presentation of gifts, but many long speeches before and after the cutting of the extravagantly decorated cake. We did not stay for the dance.

The second wedding was in a remote village and we took a long route to it, as Stephen wanted to show me the fertile hills and valleys of his region. The beautiful drive ended at a homestead at the top of a steep hill. The wedding party was not yet back from church so we waited in one of the houses until they arrived. Although these families were clearly not wealthy, about two hundred guests attended the reception; only the gifts were less lavish and the refreshment consisted of plastic cups filled with liquid *posho*, except for the wedding party and a few special guests who received sodas. On the clothes and the cake no expense had been spared, so they were similar to other weddings. Again we sat through many speeches, but had to go before the entertainment started, as it was getting dark and we were a long way from home. On the way back we stopped until well after nightfall at a large and well appointed home, where our elderly hosts were also entertaining family visitors from South Africa.

To see in the new millennium we were to go to Ishasha, to the new hotel at the foot of the escarpment near the Congo border where I had been on Christmas Day the previous year. This time we were to spend the night there. I was curious to see what progress had been made and surprised by what we found. The dining room and bar were fully operational and most of the buildings had been finished, surrounded by neat gardens and many young trees. Several of the round *bandas* with enormously high pointed roofs were already occupied when we were allocated our three. I shared with Hilda, but saw little of her after we had taken turns to 'bathe' in the splendid bathroom where the water had not yet been connected, leaving us with a basin and jerry cans as usual, though hot water was provided. Brilliant red and gold brocade bedspreads gave the bedroom an opulent Chinese appearance, though the rest of the furniture was simple and functional.

As soon as we were ready, we set off for a goat-roast at a friend's house. The home was a splendid mansion close to the Congolese border where all was peaceful under the star-bright sky. For once mine was not the only white face at the party – one of the daughters of the house had brought a German colleague home from work in Nairobi. An excellent white wine offered a delicious alternative to the beer and whiskey usually served on such occasions, as we sat chatting in the courtyard under the stars in the soft tropical night. After the barbecue, which included roast goat among other delicacies, we returned to the hotel just before midnight to see the New Year in. A raucous band was playing at the edge of an outdoor dance floor under a blue-striped awning. The few dancers and the band were hushed briefly for the stroke of midnight from the radio. A great cheer went up together with a handful of small firecrackers. Then someone passed round a few sparklers and a drop of champagne in plastic cups to our party and we all hugged and wished each other a happy new year. About twenty minutes later the band played *Auld Lang Syne,* which seemed rather incongruous – and was unfamiliar to most of those present. The halfheartedness of the dancing which followed surprised me.

'Why aren't you and your friends dancing?' I asked Hilda.

'Oh, the band is too awful. You can't dance to that music,' she replied scathingly, before retiring to the bar to watch the big television screen.

The dancers were almost exclusively men clutching beer bottles as partners, which might have been the real reason for the girls' reluctance. Deafened by the music which made it impossible to hear what anyone said, I was relieved when this bizarre experience came to an end with Margaret suggesting we go to bed shortly after one o'clock.

Sunday morning means going to church for most Ugandans, especially in the Christian west and even more so on the first day of a new year, let alone a new millennium. So we, too, expected to attend a service somewhere, but it was mid-morning before we left the hotel and there was some discussion as to where we were going. We arrived at the Church of Uganda church in one of the villages on the escarpment just as the service was ending. Stephen was keen to go in and the reason soon became clear. He made a political speech at the end of the service. Then we rushed on to the next village, where outside the Catholic church clusters of people hung at the doors of the overfilled building. This time Stephen went in alone, leaving the rest of us in the car in a minuscule patch of shade.

'I'll only be a minute,' he said, as he disappeared into the throng.

It turned into a very long minute, as once again he wished to speak and the end of the service took time to come. Meanwhile a storm blew up and it began to rain. We could either suffocate in the car with the windows shut, or get soaked with them open. The latter was more acceptable, as the sun would soon come out again to dry us off. Eventually we arrived back in Rukungiri for a snack at the Club in mid-afternoon before going home. Stephen was off again almost immediately, this time to a christening. No peace for a politician even at the most festive times!

We spent a quiet evening. Hilda's friends had to pack, as they were leaving early in the morning to go to their separate homes by bus. With some difficulty Stephen had found a lift for me with his friend Sam, the best man from the first wedding. He was already committed to taking his brother and the newly-weds with their year-old baby back to Kampala in his ancient jeep, but they squeezed up and let me sit in front. I offered to help with the driving, not least because it is more pleasant to have the wheel to hang on to on a bad road than to bounce about among the luggage.

'Thanks for the offer,' said Sam, 'but I think it's too difficult for you. It's not an easy car to drive.'

This appeared to be true to judge from the difficulty he had changing gear. Nevertheless, we reached Kampala safely, faster and in greater comfort than on public transport.

28. NIGHTMARE JOURNEY

We were not to travel in darkness
When the sun had withdrawn its light,
For the road might be threatened by robbers
Or other grim horrors of night.

I'd returned to the town at the day's end,
Worn out and in need of some food.
While I dined on *matoke* and goat stew,
Rumbling thunder made noises rude.

Soon lightning flashed on the sky line,
Black clouds rolled rapidly in;
The thunder growled louder and longer,
And rain poured with deafening din.

The lightning flashed blue on the water
Of the down-rushing rip-roaring rain;
The highway became a fierce torrent,
While a river raged wild in the drain.

I waited in patience and shelter
While the storm rolled over and on.
By the time the heavens grew calmer
The last of the daylight had gone.

The rain was now falling quite gently;
No need to fear further delay.
As I drove through the tunnel of darkness,
My headlights showed clearly the way.

Then suddenly ghosts rose before me,
Writhing spectral as mist in the night;
Slow reels they danced, swaying and swinging,
Throwing back in my eyes the car's light.

It seemed that the road was on fire
Giving rise to this smoke white as snow.
No easy way round it nor through it
As blind progress grew ever more slow.

Eyes strained in the ghastly motion
A clear point of reference to see,
But disappeared had the roadside
And every last dwelling and tree.

Then the tunnel suddenly brightened
As silver-edged clouds replaced black.
The ghosts grew shorter and thinner;
The edge of the road came back.

As I drove through a sleeping village
All the spectres were suddenly gone.
And from misty pale clouds emerging
A sliver of silver moon shone.

Thank God the nightmare was over,
No more swooping ghosts that night;
I reached home without further trouble
And gratefully switched on the light.

29. A DEATH

Birth seems a far greater problem in Uganda than death. There is no sign of family size diminishing and in spite of wars and AIDS the population is still growing, from under ten million in 1960 to over twenty million in 2000. Ordinary people do not see this as a problem.

'England is about the same size as Uganda and you have a population three times the size of ours yet you seem to manage very well. We have plenty of land. Why should we not have more people? Children are a blessing,' they say.

There are in fact very good reasons why Uganda with its agricultural economy can not sustain the same level of population as Britain. A higher standard of living is unattainable with the present rate of population increase. Families struggle to educate their children who later can not find jobs and have insufficient land to grow food, as plots get smaller through endless division. The area around the college clearly demonstrated this. It had been infested with tsetse fly until about fifty years ago. Since the flies were cleared, making it safe for human habitation, the college was built and the nearby trading centre grew into a town. Increasing numbers of people came to the area: lecturers for the college, teachers for schools, staff for a second teachers college and all the support services required by these relatively wealthy new inhabitants. Other people moved in to escape insecurity in the east. Vast tracts of bush were cleared to provide land for housing and above all fields. This was still going on, and in my two and a half years, I saw ever more scrub brought under cultivation and new houses sprouting along the roads. Trees were rapidly disappearing from the landscape with little or no effort made to replace them. The increasing scarcity of firewood, diminishing fertility of farmland and increasing drought are already making it difficult to sustain even the present population.

The AIDS crisis which had been very much in evidence during my visits in 1990 and 1994 seemed to have largely disappeared. An open and vigorous campaign of information and condom advertisements appeared to have been effective. Now AIDS was rarely mentioned, but people were no longer disappearing to funerals every few days. Although a number of students were delcted from the college lists each year, nearly all were discipline cases or unpaid fees. As far as I know, only one student died unexpectedly during teaching practice, probably not of AIDS. The blood transfusion service came round regularly. The English woman in charge told me that all the blood was screened and only about one percent was contaminated. Not all students were donors, of course, but a significant number were. Many students were in poor health for various reasons. Malaria was rampant, because the college with its dense population was surrounded by swamps. On one AIDS Awareness Day the students were offered free testing at the health centre. I asked how many students had taken advantage of the offer; the answer was two. When people requested AIDS tests at the health centre they usually turned out positive, I was told, but we lost only one staff member to suspected AIDS.

I had managed to avoid going to a funeral almost to the end of my time, but when one of the lecturers died I could not possibly plead that I did not know him, because I had passed him almost daily. A tall man, a pipe smoker and the only one with a beard, Mr. Waiswa used to sit on a low wall on my way to class, either reading the paper or just smoking his pipe. He rarely looked up and I was never sure whether I should disturb him with a greeting. He never came to the staff room, but was pleasant and friendly when there was occasion to speak. I did not notice that he looked ill at any time.

One day Apollo, one of the neighbours, came to tell me that Mr. Waiswa had died the previous night. He wanted me to take him and another member of staff to the dead man's home, because as members of the staff welfare organisation they had to make the arrangements for his burial the next day. When someone died everybody was expected to go to the funeral. This could involve travelling long distances and always seemed to take up a whole day. I ought to pay my respects, Apollo said, then I would not have to go to the funeral. My colleagues really wanted transport, so we set off in the car. When we met my nextdoor neighbour on the way looking for a *boda-boda* to go to the same place, he got in too.

The home was not far off the road north of the town. The track wound through trees and was so narrow that it was difficult to avoid the roots. At the end we found a number of small buildings scattered around an open space with a big mango tree under which about twenty men were sitting on benches. We greeted them before going to a house on the right where a cluster of women sitting on the ground outside the door were moaning quietly. Inside more women surrounded the body lying under a cloth on a mattress on the floor. Not a word was spoken as Apollo went up and lifted the sheet off the dead man's face, looked at him for a moment and then covered him again. An old woman opposite us now started wailing loudly and cradling the dead man's head. We stood with bowed heads a little longer and then went out. The old woman was the dead man's mother. His wife had left him when he became ill, angry because she suspected that he had infected her with AIDS.

We returned to the men under the tree and sat with them talking quietly. They were all speaking the local language, but I knew that Apollo did not understand much more than I did, so I asked him in a whisper what was happening. I also wondered if I should not be sitting with all the other women on the ground.

'Certainly not,' he said, to my relief, 'your place as a lecturer is here with us. We are waiting for more relatives to arrive before we can make the arrangements for the burial tomorrow.'

The funeral Mass was to be said at this house at midday and then as many people as possible would go to his true home much further north in the county. Transport as usual was a problem, even though they could use the college lorry. We sat in silence a little longer and then left.

'Should I go to the funeral?' I asked, not keen to spend the next day attending incomprehensible rites which were likely to take all day. I was also selfishly worried about having to fill my car with people and take it miles over rough roads. I did not go, but afterwards, when people asked why I was not there, I felt that perhaps I should have gone.

A few months later I did finally attend a burial.

Coffins for sale with household furniture at the roadside

30. JAMES AND HIS GRANDMOTHER'S FUNERAL

Before Paul went off to boarding school, at a time when Angela and James were at home as well, these young people wanted to take me to their village. I was a bit wary of these visits to remote spots at the end of bad tracks, but they assured me that it was not far and the road was quite good. One sunny afternoon I went to their home at the coffee factory to pick up James, Angela and Paul for this outing. Little Mary wanted to come too, but the older ones would not take her. The village was quite far, but the road reasonably good. Even when we left the proper road, the track was used fairly regularly and as it was dry, only the clouds of red dust were a nuisance.

The home consisted of a number of houses with swept areas between them, surrounded by banana trees, maize fields and patches of bush and bigger trees. The new family house was a four-bed-roomed brick shell, partly roofed with corrugated iron, and with the floors of two rooms concreted. Some of the windows had shutters, but others were still open to the elements. Much work still needed to be done, but like most people, Ruth built a little as and when money became available. This had been their father's home and his mother had a smaller house behind the new one; a sister lived a little to the right and two uncles had families in some further houses to the left, one or two so small that they only contained one or two bedrooms. In between were kitchens and stores. Grandmother, a wrinkled little old woman in a worn *busuti*, was sitting on the ground sorting beans when we arrived. She greeted us warmly, but then returned to her work. We went to see their father's grave a little way behind the house, beside their grandfather's. The importance of being buried at their proper family home in the village was so great that professional people who lived and worked in the big towns often bought a plot and built a house in their home area just to have a final resting place. This accounted for a some of the smart houses found in remote spots. The new graves were large concrete slabs, a recent, and to my mind, undesirable custom. Especially where a household had been badly affected by AIDS and a number of people had died this meant an increasing area of concrete slabs taking up good land near the houses.

The young people then showed me some of their fields round the houses, before we met the other relations and sat about and talked for a little while. When it was time to go, we were all given a little gift of home grown popcorn.

James did not get much practical experience on his motor mechanics course. Although he worked in a garage where lorries were repaired during his holidays, he learned very little about cars. Steady and conscientious worker that he was, I hoped to find an apprenticeship for him in Kampala. A friend came with me to try and persuade Toyota to give him a chance. The manager promised to do his best once James had finished his course and passed his exams. By this time I would no longer be in the country, so one weekend, I took James to Kampala to introduce him to my friend and show him where the workshop was. He spent the first night with us, but then went to his uncle. I had visited the uncle's house once with Ruth, but James had never been there and, although it was on a main road, we had considerable difficulty finding it, as I could not remember the exact spot and there are no house numbers or names.

The next afternoon James reappeared unexpectedly at my friend's house together with his uncle.

'We have just had a message that my grandmother has died. I must go back at once,' James told us.

'I am sorry,' I said, 'but what can we do? It will soon be dark and I'm not driving through the forest at night. When is the funeral? Can we go in the morning?'

'They will wait with the burial until I come. I am the eldest male in the family and I must be there. Can we get there by midday?' he asked anxiously.

'If you can sleep here, we can leave as soon as I have been to the bank. I've got to pick up some tree seedlings in the forest, but we should be able to make it by lunchtime.'

James collected his bag from his uncle's house and spent the night with us. We left fairly promptly the next morning. Picking up the tree seedlings made us rather dirty and I was worried that they would get too hot in the boot of the car all day; nevertheless, we decided to go straight to the village, just stopping at Ruth's house to see if anyone still needed a lift. They had all gone.

Crowds of people had already gathered when we finally arrived at the homestead. First we had to pay our respects to the dead woman, whose body lay under a cloth in her hut. The mourners uncovered her face for a moment while we stood in silent prayer. James then rushed away on his own business. One of his sisters found me a chair in the shade under the eaves of one of the huts where various people came and talked to me for a while. Everyone seemed very busy, as food had to be prepared for all the mourners. Eventually Ruth took me to their half-built house to sit with a group of mothers and babies who were being washed and fed. I was also fed on my own on the doorstep: some fried meat and a bottle of soda. Then it was time for the burial.

The body was carried in procession to the grave, the members of the family preceding the other guests. We sat on the ground under some trees while prayers were said and speeches made about the old lady. Suddenly everybody surged forward to begin filling the grave and some old women began screaming and tearing their hair. Almost hysterical they were dragged away by relatives. This I was told was an essential part of the mourning, which I found quite disturbing. So many people crowded forward that I did not get near the grave as we had to move away first so that those at the grave side could leave.

Back at the houses I was surprised to see Martha and to discover that she was related to this family. Having been fed earlier, I was free to go now and agreed to give Martha and her parents a lift back to their house. Martha decided to come on to the town with me. She tried to explain some of the customs we had just witnessed especially the hysterical behaviour of the old ladies. It was their way of showing what a good friend they had lost, she said.

31. TREES

Uganda has wonderful trees and forests, unfortunately being diminished by the demand for fuel and farmland for the growing population. Especially along the roads the beautiful big *muvule* trees are disappearing at an alarming rate, their good hardwood often criminally reduced to charcoal for easy sale at the roadside. Around the college, scrub and bush were cleared to open up land for crops and to keep the cooking fires burning, with no thought of the future. Where children had picked sticks from the bush near my house when I first arrived the bushes had already made way for gardens and they had to go ever further for firewood. Whenever the owner of a tree was desperate for school fees or hospital treatment, another tree bit the dust despite laws intended to preserve them. Our librarian, who rented a house nearby, came in late one morning. The lovely shading *muvule* in his yard had been cut down two days before. A policeman and a forestry officer wanted to know who had given permission. In fact, the tree fellers had produced the necessary permit purporting to be from the forestry office. Who had issued it? No one could say. Villagers cut down branches from the trees beyond my garden when they had finished burning up all their own. Where would it all end? In jest I often told people to plant sweet bananas instead of *matoke*, so that they would be able to eat something when they finally ran out of wood for cooking.

'We'll use electricity then,' they said – not a realistic prospect as it was already too expensive for most people. They also moaned about climate change and increasing heat and drought, but few were aware of the connection between tree cover and rainfall. Colleagues, especially in the agriculture department, and some students did understand the problem and wanted to do something about it. In theory at least tree planting was encouraged. Finding time, money and the energy to actually do it was another matter. However, negotiations for a planting scheme for the college began in my first year. An abandoned citrus orchard could be resuscitated and a wood lot planted next to it.

Trees around the sports field would be welcomed to provide shade for supporters, although grazing cattle posed a risk for seedlings. I had begged some money in England so the financial excuse was no longer valid. Finally, with support from George, head of agriculture, and David, in charge of one of the student halls of residence, and representatives of the student council, a scheme was devised. Headed by the students in the agriculture department, each of the five halls of residence would collect the readily available seeds of acacia and *musisi* trees and raise them in special seed beds on agriculture department land. I would purchase plastic tubing and the students would gather compost. Student support for these activities was secured by making them part of their enthusiastically contested inter-hall competitions. Timing was important as planting-out needed to be done during the rainy season in March and April, so February was the time for sowing. As so often, delays in building the shade roofs and sowing meant that by the time the rain came the seeds were only just in their pots. They flourished and were well cared for until the students went home in April. The primary teachers who came in May also took good care of the now healthy lots of seedlings, but when these were ready for planting out it was exam time and no one was prepared to start digging.

After the exams everyone was away on teaching practice and by the time we came back the seedlings were trees with roots deep into the ground below their pots. They were smothered in weeds and still no one wanted to plant them out. We encouraged local people to come and help themselves, but few of the trees found homes.

Trying to set a good example, I had done some tree planting of my own: a mauve flowering jacaranda in front of the house, which did not do well, a mango and an avocado along the garden path at the back, and four *neem* trees, magic trees which are supposed to keep both termites and mosquitoes away. One of these trees died, another was not a *neem*, but a look-alike which flourished and grew much faster. The other two grew slowly. A beautiful male, and thus infertile, pawpaw tree had started to grow behind the house soon after my arrival much more successfully than the female pawpaws I planted, though I did get some fruit in the end. For a while the flowers of the male tree growing in attractive sprays were visited every evening at dusk by huge moths whose wings whirred so fast that one could hear but not see them in the failing light. Eventually one or two got trapped in the house. They had great black delta wings with little silver windows. People kept offering to cut down the male pawpaw as it was useless, but it had a lovely shape and for a while provided the best shade behind the house. In the end I had it cut, as the female one fruiting beside it was feeble and overshadowed by it.

The *neem* tree (azadirachta indica A. Juss.), a native of India, suddenly received considerable publicity and became very popular. It sounded almost too good to be true. The root system was said to keep termites away and the flowers to make mosquitoes infertile. Various other parts have medicinal and commercial uses; it grows straight, giving useful timber and its feathery leaves make it an attractive shade tree. The only drawback was that seeds and seedlings were not easy to obtain. I hope it will not lose its reputation like the pretty umbrella tree whose lacy branches growing in wheels at right angles to the stem had made it a prestigious shade tree for the grounds of grand new houses built by the rich. Rumour suddenly had it that the trees led to the death of the master of the house as soon as the roots reached the walls, with the result that many of them were hastily cut down in fear. This superstition possibly arose from a confusion with a different northern coniferous umbrella tree which grows in Russian churchyards, thus being associated with death. It is more likely that it gained credence from the fact that often the owners of such new houses had contracted AIDS and died some years after planting, but unconnected with, the trees.

The April date of my final departure was fixed very much with tree planting in mind. I still had most of the money donated for this purpose and wanted to spend it on seedlings for planting when the rains came in March, but the weather continued hot and sunny throughout this March. Ten miles away it rained and people began planting maize, but in our area the clouds remained distant and the heat unmitigated. This saddened me as I looked forward to the rains, a spring-like time when the brown fields turn green overnight and many trees burst into new leaf and blossom and the temperature drops to a more pleasant level. A practical problem with planting trees was the difficulty of digging holes in ground baked rock-hard and, even if we could have planted, watering the young trees would have been all but impossible. I was reluctant to hand over money to staff and students who were keen enough for the moment, but would their enthusiasm survive the sports and exam seasons ahead?

Some of the tree money I gave to Annet's school, where the children were already digging holes for fruit trees when I visited. For the college I brought seedlings from tree nurseries for two separate groups of students who were eager to plant. One group, on their own initiative and unknown to me, had planted three hundred eucalyptus trees the year before, but only five remained as termites had destroyed the rest. We bought *dawa,* special insecticide to dispose of the pests. This also required the removal of the ant hills, waist high mounds with intricate interiors which included gardens in which the termites cultivated a particular fungus to supplement their food supply. The queen termite has a special clay chamber of her own in which she is constantly groomed by a number of workers to keep her damp – no mean task for little termites as she is a thumb-sized squidgy white lump of an egg machine, unable to move because of her size. She is highly regarded as a delicacy by people, but I refused to taste the one unearthed next to my house, much to the delight of the man who had dug her out. The termites were also prized as food when they grew wings and flew from their mounds and holes in the ground. People particularly partial to this speciality were not keen to see termite hills destroyed, but the majority approved of their removal as this menace eats its way unseen through the insides of roots, sticks, books and anything else of less than concrete density.

The students still wanted to plant eucalyptus as it grows fast and straight and seedlings were readily available and cheap, but I persuaded them to try some other trees as well. The seedlings that I bought had to be left in a shady place where it was possible to water them until it was time to plant. I also brought sacks of coffee husks free for collection from piles behind the local coffee factory. They were tipped into a pit and kept damp. Within a few weeks they turned into rich black compost. All this had to be left until the rains started and I can only hope that the termite mounds have gone and many trees are now growing around the college.

32. KARAMOJA

Karamoja District in the northeast of Uganda is quite different from the rest of the country. It is semi-desert, rapidly turning to desert, inhabited by fierce war-like herdsmen, who have so far successfully resisted all outside attempts to change their ways. Cattle is their life and cattle raiding their sport, a rather more dangerous one now that they are using AK47s instead of spears. Physically the area is different too: rolling pale yellow land with occasional dry thorn trees and barren rocky outcrops, remnants of ancient volcanoes. The air is generally very clear so the tors and mountains are visible from fifty, even a hundred, miles away. It feels wild, spacious, untamed, exciting – and it was out of bounds to us most of the time, on account of the risk of getting in the way of a cattle raid. This had prevented us from climbing Mount Moroto early in 1998, when we had to make do with a lesser extinct and eroded volcano, Napak, on the edge of the district.

Now two volunteers were stationed at a Catholic mission hospital some way into the district and a number of friends had visited them, travelling there by bus. I wanted to drive but could find no one to go with me on the only free week end I had left. The previous week there had been an incident on the road as a result of which people had been advised not to travel. I asked in every town on the way whether it was safe. Nobody gave a straight answer, but when I asked at a garage in Soroti, the nearest big town, they said that the bus had gone up that morning, so it was probably alright. At Katakwi, the next district headquarters on the road, they said that quite a lot of traffic had passed, so most likely it was safe.

'But you can't go alone. You must take someone with you,' said the lady in the office where I had sought advice.

As nobody was waiting around for a car ride to the dangerous country, I had to ignore her advice. As I was approaching the Karamoja border, I suddenly became aware that the schools were empty. I wondered why, as it was not holiday time. Then I noticed that the homesteads were deserted too, and began to worry. At this point two men in uniform came walking along the road towards me: the oddest pair I have ever seen. One was well over six foot, the other under five, making them such a funny sight that fear was forgotten. Waving, they shouted a friendly greeting and then the tall one turned to the short one and said, 'Hurry up!' The poor little fellow was practically running already.

Before I had time to worry about the absence of people, which could only mean cattle raiding, I came to the most appalling bit of road: big sharp boulders right across the width of it. In the distance a lorry appeared. We both made such slow and painful progress that it was some time before I realised that it was coming towards me not driving in the same direction. I knew that I was close to Iriri, a trading centre where some Italian agriculturalists were stationed, so I decided to keep going and hope that the road would improve. After about a mile it did, and when I stopped to take a photo, some men in the flowing cloaks of the Karamojong accompanied by small boys strode towards the road from the nearest homestead. That was a relief. It took me some time to reach the Italians' compound, because suddenly I found myself on a beautiful, apparently unused, dirt road going back in the direction I had come. It intrigued me, as I was certain that it was not there two years before when we had come climbing here. I followed it for a few miles before turning back to look for the Italians. One of them was in and told me that I had already passed through the area from which the people had fled from the cattle raiders and the worst bit of road, so I might as well go on. When I stopped for a soda in the trading centre, a young man approached, asking if I could give his friend a lift to Moroto, the district headquarters.

'I'm not going that far,' I explained, 'but he is welcome to come with me as far as I'm going.'

The friend turned out to be the elderly medical assistant in charge of the local health centre, who needed to collect drugs from the district headquarters. He also wanted to take his daughter back to school there and – a real bonus – he spoke good

English. He proved interesting company and the last miles flew by, especially as the road was good too. At first he wanted me to drop him at the point where I had to turn off the main road, but in the end he decided to come all the way to Matani.

The mission, at the end of the row of shops which formed the trading centre, was an oasis of green trees, clean white buildings, flowering shrubs, everything neat and well-kept. The solidly-built houses had running water and electricity from a big generator, which served the whole compound. The hospital was well-equipped, clean and busy, with nurses in different coloured uniforms going quietly about their business. Gun-shot wounds were a speciality here, as the whole area was infamous for cattle raiding and tribal warfare. The young man riding his bicycle through the village, draped in a tartan wrap, with rows of coloured beads around his neck and an AK47 slung across his chest was a memorable example of what progress meant here.

There had been no rain for five months and much of the area was desert-like, with dark figures striding over the parched yellow ground, sometimes driving herds of cattle. They mostly went in the direction of a high grey wall some way off down a slope behind the mission compound. Dust clouds hung in the air around the cattle waiting there to be fed and watered from a water treatment plant clearing the effluent from the compound. Intended for watering the mission vegetable gardens, it provided vital drink for cattle, sheep and donkeys during this drought, and the special elephant grass used to clean the water also made juicy food for the starving animals. Only the goats did not seem to need the water and swarmed off elsewhere to forage. Near the church a sizable wood lot had been planted, fenced off to prevent the goats from eating the young trees. The straight stems were still thin but looked good for building poles and firewood. Nearby yellow jerry cans stretched in a row for several hundred yards as people queued to pump water from the borehole which seemed to serve a huge community.

The time with my friends passed all too quickly and soon it was Sunday morning and I had to return. Unfortunately nobody wanted a lift, but just beyond the trading centre a man on crutches flagged me down. I picked him up, thinking he would only go a little way, but to my surprise he wanted me to take him almost as far as Iriri. There I had been asked to call on two sisters. They were at church, so I too went there. As the service was about to end, a crowd had gathered outside, including a number of teachers from the school. When they heard about my plan to return on the new road I had found earlier, they said that I must get a companion. I was under the impression that one of them offered, but he only came as far as the shops with me to recruit someone else. After exhaustive enquiries he found a large old man in tattered clothes, very excited about travelling in a car. Yes, he would like to go to Namalu to visit relations; he would be delighted to come.

So we set off down the new road, my companion hanging out of the window shouting and waving to everyone we passed. When there were fewer people around he tried to make conversation in Swahili, but knowing little more than I did, we soon ran out of things to say. We passed through attractive countryside round the southern end of Napak, its rocky slopes rising on our right. Much new settlement could be seen from the road: freshly thatched huts and new fences round the homesteads. Occasionally we came across men herding cattle along the road. The first time this happened, my companion made me stop. He wanted to get out and drive the cattle off the road, but I persuaded him to stay in and he contented himself with shouting to the herdsmen. It only occurred to me later that this was why people had been anxious to find me a companion. If I had driven along as one usually would at the back of the herd and slowly through it, the herdsmen might have thought that I was attacking their cattle – with dire consequences. The other danger the old man tried to save me from was the drifts: steep descents into dry stream beds. He grabbed my left arm fiercely every time we approached one in his anxiety to make me slow down, which of course I did anyway, especially as my exhaust had come adrift some time earlier and I had no wish to lose it completely.

Gradually the trees and the homesteads thinned out as we came round the mountain and found ourselves facing Mount Moroto in the distance. This worried me as I had expected the road to run southeast not directly east, swinging round to the north, but it was not marked on any map, nor did it go straight to Namalu. It met the other main road to Moroto much further north near Nabilatuk. On this road there was occasional traffic and more habitation. The excitement of the wilderness was left behind. We picked up a mother with a sick baby and a young man who wanted to go to the dispensary in Namalu. They left me there, as did the old man, whose relations were most surprised and happy to see him.

The rest of the journey was rather tedious. It had clouded over and the road ran too close along the base of Mounts Kadam and Elgon to give a good view. The road had bad patches, so it was impossible to go fast for fear of hitting one; the noise from the exhaust was annoying and I was getting worried about the time, as I still had to pick up a student in Mbale, introduce her to her prospective practice school along the way and try to get home before dark.

We succeeded in reaching the school in daylight, but by the time the business was sorted out it was practically dark. I still took the more direct route home through the bush – the only time I ever drove any distance on murram roads through the countryside after dark. The danger in this lay more in the unpredictable potholes and occasional rocks which were difficult to spot in the headlights than in bandits. Driving required the closest attention, which was exhausting. However, we got back safely at about half past eight with a feeling of considerable satisfaction.

33. RACHEL'S LATER PROBLEMS

A very large woman in a yellow *busuti* lumbered to the door. I did not immediately recognise Rachel. I had not seen her for more than a year. She was heavily pregnant and brought an invitation to her wedding a fortnight later. I wondered whether she would still be in one piece by then, but she assured me that the baby was not due for another month. Her fiance was encouraging her to put off the wedding till after the birth.

'But I can't do that,' she said. 'What's there to make him get married once the baby has arrived? He might just never get round to the wedding.'

This was sad, but irrefutable.

Rachel had had her fair share of other troubles, too. When she had malaria and bad backache resulting from it, she had not been able to sleep. She had gone to the drug shop (pharmacy) in the village where she worked and bought *Ventolin*, an asthma drug, because she had heard that it helped you to sleep. I was horrified at such misguided self-medication and asked her never to get drugs without proper advice, especially in her condition.

'But what could I do? There was no one to ask,' she said.

In addition to her personal problems, there were difficulties with the school which her father had started and then left her to run. It was not easy to get teachers when there was little money to pay them. She was teaching English, as I had always suspected she would, but she was not trained and found it difficult to cope. I asked how she would manage with the baby. Would she get maternity leave?

'I'll manage somehow until the end of the term. Agnes will come and help me when she has finished her exams. I hope she will teach English for me until she goes to university. It'll be alright, don't worry.'

'Well, I wish you luck! And a very happy wedding! I'm sorry I won't be able to come. I'm going home for a month next week.'

I managed to send her a present and Martha's cockerel before I left. When I came back I asked her father when the baby had been born.

'Not yet,' he said every time I inquired over the next few weeks. It finally arrived in mid-November, not at her home with her mother to help, but in the next village where she lived in rented accommodation with her husband. He was away most of the time, so one of her sisters stayed with her.

Some time later I went to see her. The long school holidays had started and Agnes was staying with her. She collected me and we went together with little Milly. The baby was a bouncing little girl, at six weeks already smiling and keen to stand. This was amazing, considering that her birth had been traumatic.

Rachel, Milly and the author with Baby Charity

Because Rachel was a teacher and not permanently resident in the village, the villagers thought she was a snob and so they would not help her when she desperately needed it on the night the baby was born. It was only after much pleading that the midwife agreed to attend her and then she was not very co-operative, so there were avoidable complications after the birth. Fortunately all was well in the end, and now Rachel was able to have a bit of a rest and enjoy her dear little daughter. It had been agreed in the family that Agnes would teach English for the school next term and I would try and help her to prepare.

Just before the beginning of the new school year Rachel and baby came to visit me. Both were well, but Rachel was in trouble again – this time as the headteacher of her father's school. Inspectors were expected at the beginning of term to ensure that there was adequate classroom provision. The school did not have this and it would take too long to construct proper buildings, so she proposed putting up a temporary classroom with tarpaulins spread on poles.

'Could you possibly lend me the money for the poles? It will only be for a short time. When the children come back to school and pay their fees, I can pay you back. I've asked Daddy, but he says he has no money. And I need it now,' she explained.

She had thought everything out very carefully and planned so well, that I could hardly refuse, although the sum was large. But could I afford it? Whatever good intentions Rachel had about repayment, it seemed doubtful that she could manage it when the time came. I decided I could risk it.

'Thank you, thank you. You have saved my school. You must come and see it soon. Can you?'

'I'll try, but you know that my husband is coming to visit and we have not made any plans yet. I'd like to see it very much.'

A few weeks later David and I managed to visit the school without warning at a weekend. It was not easy to find nor to recognise it as a school when we got there: a tumble-down jerrybuilt shell, which had been used as a school before. Most rooms had rubble floors and the ceilings, black with damp, looked ready to fall. The only indication that they served as classrooms were the blackboards on the walls. Only three rooms had doors. One was an office with a table and chair and even a cupboard, the other two contained some chairs. The 'temporary classroom' at the back provided the barest shelter. Piles of bricks and stones overgrown with weeds littered the site, making it hazardous to walk about. Rachel had gone home for the weekend, and I was quite glad that she did not see our reaction to her school. Yet it had passed the inspection!

Not long after this Rachel came and – very much to my surprise and delight – returned the money I had lent her. Her troubles, however, were not over. The landlord demanded the whole year's rent in advance after only three months. She could not pay this and the teachers' salaries unless the parents paid the fees promptly, which never happened, and under no circumstance could she pay two terms in advance. She tried to negotiate with the landlord, who would accept no excuses from her, so she had to get the village chief to plead with him. None of this was easy for a young woman in a country where women were still expected to kneel before men and not to argue with them. I tried to persuade her father to deal with this business, as he was the owner of the school and it was his fault that she was experiencing all these difficulties. He just smiled and said,

'Oh, yes. But I'm very busy.'

I am certain that he did nothing. As I was leaving the country for good at this point I could do no more to help either.

Some months later I received this letter from Rachel:

'You left when the landlords were on my back but somehow I managed. I talked to Daddy but still he had no money. When I went back to the school, I found the landlord at my place very cross!!! I had to deceive him in order to cool his temper. After three weeks the man came back. When I saw him I had to hide away from him. By good chance I met four parents. They had brought school fees. I was very happy; in fact, God rescued me. I gave him (the landlord) all that money and I told him that I would be giving him some every month. At first he refused and I was not keen either, as I had not yet paid the teachers' salaries. I talked to the teachers to excuse me up to the second term. Generally I had a very rough time. Maybe that's why I had the severe malaria and headache.

We have begun the new term. The students' turn-up is somehow pleasing and I'm getting some new students also, *though still payment of school fees is very poor. Most parents are farmers and the season this year has totally changed. Some (people) are still planting and others harvesting.**

Measles attacked the baby and she was on six hours' treatment, but she is also recovering now she has the rash on her body.

I'll have to end here. I'm going to school.

---

*Footnote: The rains which were due to start in March had not materialised.

34. UNFINISHED FINALE

Time passes all too quickly and even the best laid plans rarely work out as intended. My plan to return to England in April was intended to give me the beginning of the rainy season in March for tree planting and to allow me to teach almost to the end of the second term which marked the end of the year's formal classes for the secondary teachers. Exams took place on their return to college in June immediately followed by teaching practice. Originally the primary teachers' exams were to be in May, so their classes should have finished in February, but another term had recently been added to their course. This was particularly frustrating as the marking of their visual aids, an area in which I had suggested some fairly radical changes, would now take place in May. The staff meeting in preparation for this, which I was most anxious to attend, was also postponed again and again, so I could only hope that time spent persuading various lecturers individually of the benefits of the changes had not been wasted.

Leaving my garden, on which I had lavished interest and care, was easier than expected as it had suffered from the prolonged dry season. In the front garden, the bananas were doing quite well and I had harvested a small bunch, but the prolific loofah plant had dried up and the passion fruit vine, having grown up to the roof, suddenly shed most of its leaves. A wild passion fruit had spread all over the back of the house the previous year, but had burnt up in that hot season. It had regenerated slowly to cover much of the wall, but it did not produce a single fruit, while the grafted one at the front bore plenty. A hedge of red-leafed hibiscus, which had grown and flowered attractively for months, also seemed to have reached the end of its life. I knew that everything would be cut down as soon as I left, because people liked to keep the ground round the houses bare for fear of snakes and possibly other creatures. The rats came in anyway, as did chickens, ducks and cats occasionally. Once I found a small tortoise in the front garden and for a while a black toad, which I mistook for a piece of coal until it blinked at me, lived in a certain spot under a shrub. Toads came out after dark during the rains, scaring me by suddenly hopping away from under my feet when I harvested the water from the roof, but I never saw a snake anywhere near the houses, not even one of the jumping snakes for which the area was renowned.

Remarkable changes had taken place in the college in the two and a half years I spent there. Some improvements had been made for the graduation in my first year, when the outside of the offices was repainted and a modern concrete statue erected near the entrance. Later several classrooms were refurbished: the holes in the floor were repaired while louvre windows replaced the glass-less rusty old frames. The staffroom was floored with vinyl tiles and newly furnished, mainly with comfortable chairs to replace the huge, hard, heavy wooden ones. A larger generator was briefly installed to keep the library, some classrooms and the security lights on during power shedding, the regular evening cuts in the electricity supply. This itself was due to end soon as the new power plant in Jinja was nearing completion. One of the staff houses, which were all desperately dilapidated, had been refurbished and others were to follow. Student numbers continued to rise, with four hundred primary teachers in the first year English course when I left compared to a previous maximum of two hundred and forty. The opposite had happened with the secondary teachers who had gone down from twenty three to nine students. Specialisation in all National Teachers Colleges, which had been discussed for years, was about to take place, though it was difficult to see how this could be properly implemented. Change was always in the air and a sense of impermanence seemed endemic, as staff could be transferred or made redundant and courses altered at a moment's notice.

When the time came for me to leave it was hard to realise that this strange period of my life was over. My mind was still full of the day-to-day concerns about my friends and my work, tasks unfinished and problems unresolved. For months after my return to Britain my thoughts were in Uganda as much as at home. Letters rarely satisfied my curiosity as my most burning questions remained unanswered. On the other hand, it was easier to ignore the requests for financial assistance. Although life in Uganda was trying at times, it taught me a great deal about myself and other people, about my culture and theirs: so different on the surface and yet quite similar at heart. The pace of life was slower – possibly because of the heat – but somehow it seemed more fully lived. Real lives were shared and provided the day-to-day interests and excitement, and as yet there was none of the smudging of the borders between reality and fiction, which now characterises English television-dominated lives. I miss the understanding way people look you in the eye and readily share a joke even with a total stranger. I shall always look back on this period of my life with pleasure and gratitude for all the hospitality, kindness and friendship of the many people who shared their lives with me.

> And so goodbye, dear money tree,
> Go back now to your own country,
> Where you no more will shaken be
> By those who want your gifts for free.
> May peace, joy and prosperity
> Be theirs who have so troubled thee.
>
> But better still by far 'twould be
> If they themselves would plant a tree;
> By using each his own ability,
> The total strength of the community,
> To set themselves for ever free
> From wretched want and poverty.
>
> May those who have prosperity
> Share it with those they can not see,
> Seek justice always, and equality,
> So that the whole wide world may be
> A better place for them and me.

My front garden after two years with banana tree and passion fruit vine

GLOSSARY

banda	rustic round hut for tourist accommodation.
boda-boda	bicycle, or increasingly motor scooter, where the passenger sits on padded carrier or passenger seat.
bounce	Ugandan expression for calling on someone who is out.
Busuti or gomes(i)	dress with high puff sleeves, square neck and yards of material tied with a wide brocade belt worn by married women, first in Buganda, but now regarded as national dress.
dawa	Swahili: medicine.
kanzu	long white overshirt worn by men on festive occasions.
malwa	locally brewed millet beer, consumed with long straws from a communal pot.
murram	red clay used for surfacing secondary roads – firm but dusty when dry, slippery when wet.
muvule	enormous hard-wood trees common in Eastern Uganda, but not easy to propagate. I could not find any seedlings.
muzungu	Swahili general term for white people, also used as a form of address mainly by children.
posho	maize porridge, usually solid and rather tasteless, the cheapest staple food, generally served with bean sauce to all students.
soda	non-alcoholic bottled fizzy drink with different flavours produced and marketed by the Coca-Cola and Pepsi companies.

waragi   strong gin-like spirit distilled from bananas.

This book is privately published and obtainable from:

SUGARBROOK BOOKS
Ingrid Pasteur
Woodland House
24 Greenaway Lane
Hackney
Matlock DE4 2QB
Tel. 01629 735956

Price £8.95 including P+P
Cheques made payable to Sugarbrook Books

£1 for every copy sold and any eventual profit will go to support the people in the book who still need financial assistance.